Connecting with God

Jude Levermore

illustrated by
Simon Smith

The Bible Reading Fellowship
OPENING THE BIBLE

 Contents

With thanks to my husband, Phil, and the confirmation group who field-tested the material for me:
Lucy Kinchin, Jenny Blackwell, Michelle Cline, Alison Bold, Michael Bold, Robin Rudd, Jackie Edwards and Wilf Merttens.

Text copyright © 1997 Jude Levermore
Illustrations copyright © 1997 Simon Smith

The author asserts the moral right to be identified as the author of this work

Published by
The Bible Reading Fellowship
Peter's Way, Sandy Lane West, Oxford OX4 5HG, England
ISBN 0 7459 3516 8
Albatross Books Pty Ltd
PO Box 320, Sutherland, NSW 2232, Australia
ISBN 0 7324 1563 2

First edition 1997
10 9 8 7 6 5 4 3 2 1 0

Acknowledgments
Scripture is taken from the Good News Bible published by The Bible Societies/HarperCollins Publishers Ltd UK © American Bible Society, 1966, 1971, 1976, 1992

A catalogue record for this book is available from the British Library

Printed and bound in Malta by Interprint Ltd

Introduction

First of all a big thank you for reading this introduction! I know how tempting it can be to skip it in order to get straight in to the course. But taking time to prepare everything thoroughly and spending time to prepare yourself will save you time in the long run!

This course is arranged in sessions. Each session is designed to cover one aspect of the basics of Christian faith. You can use the course in several ways: as a preparation for confirmation, as an introduction to the Christian faith, or you could just pick out the sessions which are relevant for whatever you happen to be doing with your regular group. Most of the sessions stand alone, although there is occasional cross-reference which is indicated in the session introduction.

Each session is divided into sections:

First Connections
Deals with how to introduce the session topic.

Bible Connections
Focuses on the topic through a specific Bible passage.

Further Connections
Helps the group to apply the Bible passage to their own lives.

Connecting with God
Presents the opportunity to respond to the challenge of the session.

The Big Question
Gets to the heart of the matter.

Concluding Connections
Provides suggestions for drawing the session together in prayer, worship and reflection, and invites the group members to make a personal and private response to God.

Each session follows the same pattern, providing a feeling of continuity, but also aims to present different approaches to studying the Bible and to exploring our relationship with God.

We have called the worksheet for each session *Personal Connections Sheet*. The two pages of each sheet need to be photocopied back to back, providing each group member with an A5 leaflet which will build session by session into a record of their experience of the course. The sheets provide the group members with an extension of the session theme to reflect on between each session. You'll find each one includes the Bible passage for the session, activities and liturgies where appropriate, and a space for them to record their private reflections between sessions. You don't have to run the course on a weekly basis if that doesn't suit you. I tend to run my courses fortnightly, as I find this allows me optimum space in my week for planning the next session. There are no allusions to 'next week' in the text so you are free to programme the sessions whenever suits you.

A few thoughts on running the sessions: first, remember that the way you behave towards the group speaks louder than the words you use. In other words you are the message you send. If you treat group members with respect, with integrity and love, then the message you send will show God in a positive light. The frightening fact is that God will be judged on how you act and it is vital that you are seen to be friendly, approachable and caring. In practical terms that means being committed to the group, learning and using their names, giving lifts home if necessary, allowing them to use the phone to contact parents, giving generously of your time, resources and chocolate cake! It is about going the extra mile and it reaps huge benefits. It means you learn as much from the group as they learn from you. If you can see the course as a time of growth for you as well as your group members your attitude will be that of servant as well as teacher. Make Jesus your model.

Secondly, be confident! You may not know all the answers—none of us does—but we know a God who does! Young people respond best to positive thinking, so make a concerted effort to banish negative speech and thoughts. This applies particularly to what might be called 'discipline problems'. If members of your group are intent on being disruptive I would advise you to respond positively. Try not to adopt an authoritarian approach, rather allowing a diversion if it will help to settle the group and then moving swiftly on to the subject in hand. Bear in mind that often the reason young people are disruptive is because they are bored, so try to discern when it is time to move on to a fresh activity. Interruptions will do no harm if you remain in control. Above all, be interested in their lives and don't allow yourself to be pushed out of the conversation.

Finally, enjoy yourself! Your group will know if your heart isn't in it. Arrange for members of your church family to pray for the group, pray yourself before you start each session and don't neglect your own spiritual well-being.

My prayer is that this course will help your young people to connect with God in a new and exciting way.

Have fun!

Connecting with Each Other

This session aims... to introduce the group members to each other, and to you as their leader. It is designed to help each individual within the group to see themselves as created by God with body, mind, emotions and spirit.

Before the session starts... prepare yourself by reading the material you will be using in the session. Prayerfully read through the Bible passage.

Prepare the room you will be using for the session, creating as warm and relaxed an atmosphere as you can. Have ready A4 folders/clip files and pencils and the Personal Connections Sheets for each member of the group, plain A4 sheets of paper and spare Bibles (all Bible passages in this course are taken from the Good News Bible).

First Connections

Welcome each group member and explain that this session is going to be an introduction to the course. Go on to say that you will be giving everybody the opportunity at the end of the session to say whether they think the course is for them. Briefly outline what will be happening in the ten sessions, adding that this is a chance for them to find out about God and that you will be giving them the time and space to work out what they believe and to check that out with what the Bible says. You'll be looking at what the Church believes and helping them to decide whether or not to stand up as a fully-fledged member of both their local church, and the Church as the body of Christ in the world, and *be* a Christian.

Explain about the Personal Connections Sheets that you will be using each week (see the Introduction on page 3). Give out the folders you have bought for your group to clip their pages into. For the group I worked with, I used a large and fairly cheap stationers to purchase a selection of A4 folders or files, in different patterns (avoiding cartoon characters or film photos, as these date so quickly) and choosing abstract patterns or plain colours, rather than the old-fashioned dark green cardboard type. I then let each member of the group choose their own folder from the selection. Obviously, not everyone got exactly what they

wanted, but it made the point that I was going to treat them as individuals and it showed them I cared enough to have bought them attractive folders. It also conveyed the thought that they would be able to make their own decisions during the course.

Follow on from your welcome and introduction with the following game:

Explain that they are each going on a journey—it can be anywhere in the universe. Cost is irrelevant—they have an unlimited amount to spend. Give out the Personal Connections Sheets for Session One, which include the journey game, and explain that they need to answer each of the questions. I suggest you also read out each question, giving the group time to write down each answer. This gives a better group feel, as the whole group are doing the activity together, filling in each question at the same time. It also helps with anyone who finds reading a difficulty—it is best not to assume that just because young people are in a mainstream school that they are competent readers.

When everyone has completed their journey, gather in the sheets and clip them together in your own file. Then, without indicating whose is whose, read them out, inviting people to guess who wrote which journey. Don't forget to include your own. It can be very revealing guessing whose was whose. I expect yours was fairly easily to detect—young people can usually spot adult answers with no trouble at all!

This exercise can tell you all sorts of things about your group. They might have drawn on a previous holiday experience, perhaps wanting to go back to somewhere they had been before. Or perhaps they highlighted people that matter to them, their attitude to their parents, money or music. They will have provided you with a variety of clues that may help you to tailor the course to their needs. Don't forget to make a mental note of anything that strikes you which may help you to encourage the individual members of your group.

As you discuss the different journeys, make sure you make positive comments and encourage the group to do the same. Say things like, 'Wow, that's a good idea—I wish I'd thought of going to Honolulu and taking a surf board—that sounds great!' or, 'Oh, clever to want to meet the angel Gabriel—he'd be able to catch me out when I get the Bible references wrong!' You know the sort of thing! Remember that primarily you are trying to put the members of your group at their ease, give them a good time and make them feel valuable to the group. That way they'll come back next time, and be relaxed and open to what you are exploring with them.

Return their sheets to them at the end of the game.

First Connections

Bible Connections

Psalm 139:1–6, 13–18

Tell the group that in every session you will be looking at a Bible passage which will help them to understand the subject under discussion. Explain that the Bible is the book of God's people and that Christians use it as a 'living document' to help them in their daily lives.

This week we are going to look at how God cares about every part of us, and knows about every part of us. We are using Psalm 139 to help us to understand this. The passage is printed on the Personal Connection Sheets. You may need to explain that the Psalms can be found in the middle of the Bible. They are a collection of prayers, songs and poems, using the full range of emotions to express faith in God. Remind the group that these writings are amazingly old and, as they weren't originally written in English, they don't seem to rhyme or appear very song-like to us. They were created by people who were very close to God. They communicated with God through their writing and knew that God cared very much for them as individuals and as a nation.

Read the passage yourself, or invite a member of your group to read it (someone you know likes to read). Alternatively, you could ask someone in your church to record all the Bible passages used in the course onto an audio cassette. You might know of a couple of people with good speaking voices who would be prepared to do this for you. It is a helpful

way of breaking up the session if you are able to use a different voice on tape and it can help your young people to concentrate. They will often listen more readily to a voice on a tape: it gives them variety and holds their interest.

When the passage has been read, go on to explain that in every session there will be time for discussion, giving them the opportunity to say what they think and to learn from each other. The discussion for this session will explore the approach to God seen in this Psalm. Kick off the discussion by asking the group whether they think about God in the same way as the writer of the Psalm. The Psalmist sees God as being very close to all that he does—as a presence that is always with him. Do the group think of God in that way? Or are there times when God seems far away? Perhaps they are aware that there are times—more often than not—when they just don't think about God at all? Be prepared to be able to give your own answers to the questions you pose and to talk about how you feel, but be careful not to burden your group with any insecurities you may have. This is a time for them, not you, so only be as honest as is helpful to them as a group. Try to listen to what they have to say, rather than doing all the talking yourself.

Further Connections

Look at the passage again, concentrating on verses 13 and 14. Explain that many Christians believe that God made each one of us with four different but complementary parts: body, mind, emotions and spirit. Write the four words on separate pieces of A4 paper in capital letters with a marker pen. Ask the members of the group to suggest a definition for each word—some are more obvious than others! Write the suggested definitions down under each heading. For example:

BODY: physical bits that make up me.

MIND: my brain, what I think, what I know.

EMOTIONS: how I feel, when I laugh, cry etc., a response to something I feel.

SPIRIT: a sense of awe, sometimes at nature or in church. A sense of right and wrong. Intuition. Just knowing inside that God wants me to do something.

Invite members of the group to write their own definition on their Personal Connections Sheets. Make it clear that the definitions you have decided upon are your personal thoughts, and that others may feel differently.

Now look at the list of activities on the Personal Connections Sheets and, in small groups of two or three, discuss which part of our make-up is involved in each activity.

Allow a few minutes for the small groups to discuss this and then call the groups together. Invite each group to contribute their thoughts on which activity involves which part of them: their body, their mind, their emotions, their spirit, or a combination of the different parts. Challenge them gently to justify their answers. Give them lots and lots of positive feedback and encouragement about their answers.

Connecting With God

Now recap your starting point. Do the group think that God knows each of them as individuals? Knows them collectively as a group? Knows about their body, their mind, their emotions and their spirit? Do they believe that God made them? Christians believe that God gave each of us a spiritual side so that we could respond to him, and that when we respond to him he sends his Spirit to live within us. Discuss together the thoughts that arise from the recap.

It would be helpful to relate a short story or anecdote at this point to help consolidate the connections with God you are helping them to make. You may want to use a personal story about how you responded to God, or use a story about a member of your church, known to your group. Alternatively, you could relate a story about a famous contemporary Christian, or use the example below which is an extract from the journal of John

Wesley (1703–91) (you may have to explain the unfamiliar language):

24 May 1738

In the evening I went very unwillingly to a society in Aldersgate Street, where someone was reading Luther's preface to the Epistle to the Romans. About a quarter before nine, while he was describing the change which God works in the heart through faith in Christ, I felt my heart strangely warmed. I felt I did trust Christ, Christ alone for salvation and an assurance was given me that He had taken away my sins...

This extract demonstrates how the spiritual side of a person's make-up can respond to God's Spirit through hearing his word. It changed John Wesley's life and he subsequently became the founder of the Methodist movement.

The Big Question

You will now have reached the point in the session when it is time to explore the crucial question. Here it is:

Are we as individuals and as a group prepared to allow our spirits to respond to God?

Explain that this question is the central point of what the course is about—letting God show us how he wants us to live our lives. Go on to reassure the group that if they would like more information about anything that is raised during the course, then you'll try to ensure it is provided—if you don't have the answer to their questions yourself, then find someone who can help. Reiterate the fact that the course is designed to help them to think through some difficult issues together, and to make some connections with each other and with God.

Concluding Connections

Explain that each session will end with a time aimed at helping the group to connect with God and each other in practice; a time of being open to God to allow him to draw near to us and teach us by his Spirit. It's a time to reflect on the session in God's presence.

For this first session keep the reflection time very short, but don't miss it out. The time you spend together as a group reflecting on what God has been saying to you during the session is of paramount importance. I know from personal experience that the times I have skimped on this important part of the session have in some way impaired the session as a whole. A time of quiet reflection roots all that has happened in God. It serves to remind the group before they leave of all they have done in the session and, most importantly, it allows God to speak directly to each individual member of the group.

I have drawn on different ideas for the time of reflection in each session of the course to model different ways of communicating with God in prayer and worship.

Invite the group to close their eyes and to re-run their day quietly in their minds: getting up in the morning, school, college, whatever, lunch, home, coming here. What emotions did they experience at different points during the day? Were they happy, sad, angry? What about experiences they might have responded to spiritually? In the quiet, invite your group to let their spirits connect with God. After a short pause quietly re-read the passage from Psalm 139.

Finish the reflection with a short prayer, ending with the word 'Amen'.

Ensure the session has a really positive ending. Provide refreshments at this point (if that is what you've decided to do) and give a good positive send-off and a warm invitation to the next session.

PERSONAL CONNECTIONS SHEET

Psalm 139:1–6, 13–18

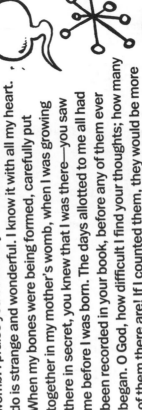
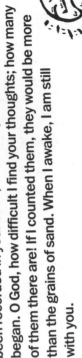

Lord, you have examined me and you know me. You know everything I do; from far away you understand all my thoughts. You see me whether I am working or resting; you know all my actions. Even before I speak, you already know what I will say. You are all around me on every side; you protect me with your power. Your knowledge of me is too deep; it is beyond my understanding. You created every part of me; you put me together in my mother's womb. I praise you because you are to be feared; all you do is strange and wonderful. I know it with all my heart. When my bones were being formed, carefully put together in my mother's womb, when I was growing there in secret, you knew that I was there—you saw me before I was born. The days allotted to me all had been recorded in your book, before any of them ever began. O God, how difficult I find your thoughts; how many of them there are! If I counted them, they would be more than the grains of sand. When I awake, I am still with you.

One

Fold here

PERSONAL REFLECTIONS

The personal reflection this week is about the crucial question:

Are we as individuals and as a group prepared to allow our spirits to respond to God?

Over the week think about what your answer to this will be.

This back page of your Personal Connections Sheet is for you to write down your questions and feelings each week. No one need see it unless you show them. It will help you to see how you and God get on over the weeks and, when you have finished the course, you will be able to look back on all that has happened. You could write it as a letter to a friend, a prayer, or just notes, but, if you can, address it to God.

CONNECTING VERSE

Come near to God, and he will come near to you.

James 4:8

FURTHER CONNECTIONS

Definitions

Body is...

Mind is...

Emotions are...

Spirit is...

Which of these do you use in the following?

- Eating a meal with friends
- Going to a music concert
- Smiling
- Praying
- Dancing
- Writing a song
- Playing football
- Kissing your girl/boyfriend

THE INCREDIBLE JOURNEY

Where would you go? It can be anywhere in the universe, in heaven, or on earth!

What method of transport would you use? Remember it doesn't matter how long the journey takes, you have all the time you want.

Who would you take with you? It can be anyone living or dead, famous or just known to you.

You can take one cassette to play on your Walkman. What will it be?

What is the one thing you absolutely must have in your suitcase? Be specific, is it your teddy bear called Jessica, a pair of new shoes that you couldn't leave behind, a poster you just love, whatever.

What or who would you miss most if you were away for a long time?

Connecting with God the Creator

This session aims... to look at the roots of the Christian faith, to get an overview of the early history of faith and to discuss its relevance today.

Before the session starts... prepare yourself by reading the material you will be using in the session. Prayerfully read through the Bible passage.

Prepare the room you will be using for the session. Have ready pencils and the Personal Connections Sheets for this session for each member of the group, plain A4 sheets of paper and spare Bibles. You'll also need one large sheet of paper, a variety of colour magazines (for example, Sunday supplements), glue sticks and some scissors, and a hole punch for putting the collages into the folders at the end of the session.

First Connections

Welcome the group and briefly recap any points that were raised in the last session. Briefly outline the theme of this session.

Place a chair in the middle of the group—a kitchen chair made of wood is best. Ask the group if they know who made it. What kind of person might have made it? What materials did they use? What tools? Make a list together of everything needed to make the chair. Then place a leaf, a horse chestnut, a flower or something similar on the chair. What was needed to make that? What kind of person might have made it? Write a similar list for the leaf—or other object.

Make the point that there is a difference between making and creating. Making means taking something that already exists and changing it to form something else. It might be useful or beautiful, but it existed before in another form. Creating means bringing into being something that never existed before.

Bible Connections
Genesis 1:1—2:4

This session uses the book of Genesis to explore the background of our faith. Genesis paints a picture of how God has connected with his world, how he has shaped history and how his chosen people have taken faith on board, struggled with it, lived by it, and kept it alive.

Explain that you're going to tell a story—probably the greatest story ever told. It might be appropriate before you begin to give a little of the background of storytelling. In the traveller tradition oral stories are still seen as very important. They are the means by which the history and values of a people are communicated and kept alive through the successive generations. There is a saying which claims that when you tell a story, standing looking over your shoulder is the person who told that story to you. They are listening to your telling of their story and, if you stray from the details, they will jab you in the ribs! In a story like the one you are about to relate thousands of people have been involved in the telling of it over the years. A vivid picture is painted when you imagine them looking over the shoulder of the person who they told—they form a line stretching back and back into time, back to the nineteenth century, back to the time when printing was invented, back to monks in the Middle Ages, back to Roman times, back to the time of Jesus and beyond that back to the time when the people of Israel were slaves in Egypt, back even beyond that to when ancient nomadic tribes sat around campfires telling stories.

This is the story they told: 'In the beginning, when God created the universe, the earth was formless and desolate. The raging ocean that covered everything was engulfed in total darkness...' (Genesis 1:1–2).

Explain to your group how this ancient story about how the universe was created reveals the nature of God the Creator—his love of beauty and order, of colour and diversity. What an amazing and mighty God we have!

Continue to read Genesis 1, through to Genesis 2:4. Don't forget to use the tape if you have one, or to invite members of the group to read for you if you feel they want to.

Bible Connections

Further Connections

When you have finished reading the passage, spend a few minutes thinking about this story of creation and then go on to show the group how the story develops from this point.

You need the large sheet of paper for this activity. Start by asking the group if they know any of the stories which appear in the book of Genesis. Write their suggestions on the sheet of paper. Don't worry if your group don't come up with the stories in the right order—you can slot them into the right order as you write them down. (The contents outline in the Good News Bible will give you the correct order.) Try to ensure that you end up with something similar to this, but primarily ensure that

you encourage the group to feel that they have contributed the bulk of the information. If you are working with a group of young people unfamiliar with the Bible, as I usually am, don't worry. By prompting them and encouraging them to use a Bible you can help them to build the list of stories—even if they haven't heard of them before (and at the same time build their confidence). You'll know how much detail you can ask from your group—I suggest you aim for about four stories, for example, Noah, Abraham, the tower of Babylon and Jacob. Don't get bogged down—an overview is what you're aiming for.

When you've finished filling in the sheet, invite your group to give their thoughts about what these stories show us about our faith, and about the way we can connect with God.

Connecting With God

The people in the stories in Genesis were constantly working out what they thought God was like. They didn't have Jesus or the record of his life to show them how to connect with God—they had to work it out for themselves. Sometimes it feels a bit like that for us, but we need to remember that we have so much more than they did to help us: our Bibles give us an accurate record of Jesus' life

and ministry and, through his Holy Spirit, we have him with us today. The people of Genesis, with the lessons they learnt and the struggles they faced, shaped the faith that has been passed down to us. We have much to learn from them about connecting with our creator God.

Kick off the discussion by exploring the picture painted in Genesis of God creating the world and everything in it, including us. What do the group think about this story of creation? How is God described in this account? Go on to explore the concept that the creating energy of God is around us all the time, causing the wind to blow, the rain to fall, babies to be born, water to flow over waterfalls, our bodies to grow and mature and so on. Take the discussion deeper by looking at the belief that God is a God who loves us, who thinks that we are of great value, who knows what we need better than we do ourselves. He is a God who grieves when we turn our backs on him and go our own way, but who loves us enough never to destroy us (use the story of Noah here by way of illustration—we might cause our own destruction, but God will never cause our destruction in the same way again). Explore the fact that God demands faithfulness and obedience from us and rewards our efforts (use the story of Abraham to illustrate this). Discuss how God is our judge and

will punish those who turn their back on him (the Tower of Babylon illustrates this), but who leads and helps his people (refer to Jacob here). Finally discuss how God demonstrates his concern for us and expects us to show concern for others (Joseph illustrates this point). At each stage of your exploration draw out the ways in which God is, or can be, described in each story.

This exercise is quite a 'thinky' school-like session, so try to keep it as light as possible. The aim is to give an overview of God's involvement with humankind, rather than an in-depth study of each individual story.

The Big Question

You have now reached the point in the session where you are ready to ask the crucial question, which is:

What is God like?

Invite your group to call to mind the descriptive words of God which came to light in the Genesis stories. For example: creative, loving, mighty, demanding our obedience, concerned for our welfare.

Hand out the colour magazines (any sort will do, though Sunday supplements seem to be the best). Explain that the task is to find a picture or an image for some of the words on their list which describe God, and to make a collage. They can tear or cut out of the magazines any image which portrays the word for them—a picture, or even just a swirl of colour which they feel evokes the adjective concerned. When they have chosen their images, give each member of the group a piece of A4 paper and ask them to arrange their pictures on the paper. Dark coloured paper, black or blue, seems

most effective but any strong colour will do. (You can use white if you can't get hold of coloured paper, but it isn't quite as effective.) Glue sticks can be passed around when everyone has finally decided on their images and where they want them to go on their sheet of paper. I suggest you give a fixed time limit to this exercise. It is important for your young people to realize that God calls for an emotional response from us, not just a head-knowledge of him, so encourage them to use their emotions when choosing their images. For instance, an idea might not necessarily be conveyed in the most obvious picture—it could be an image that evokes the feeling. Make sure you make it clear that there are no right or wrong choices in the images they select and that it is meant to be a personal choice between them and God. Invite the group to clip their collages into their folders—you'll need them for Session Seven.

Concluding Connections

Place the sheets of paper together on the floor where everyone can see them. Explain that you are going to use them as a means of worship. You may need to say a few words about what worship is: a response that comes from us when we call to mind all that God is. We cannot help but worship God when we think of all his characteristics. The images the group have chosen point to how they feel about God as individuals. Looking at them together can help them as a group to realize how great God is in all his diversity and to connect with the amazing fact that the God who created the universe also cares for each one of us as individuals. It may be appropriate to get the group to sit down around the pictures, to scatter some leaves amongst them, and to light some nightlights or candles and place them in and around the pictures. You might like to play some music—choose a piece with no lyrics, or with a simple repeating lyric, perhaps a Taizé chant of praise. While the music is playing explain that you are going to use this time to praise God for all that he is and all that he has done, using the words that your group has chosen images for. You can do this either by your saying, 'Thank you God that you are...' (and adding a word that your group has chosen), or by encouraging the group to say out loud, 'Thank you God that you are...' (followed by each of them choosing a word that is important to them).

You might like to finish this time of worship by saying this prayer:

Lord, how can we ever thank you enough
for all that you are,
for all that you have done?
We praise you for the wonder
of all that lives
and grows.
We praise you for pattern and order,
the complex and the simple.
The whole universe reflects your glory.
From the wideness of space,
to the detail of cells;
from the rainbow to the raindrop,
from the frog to the whale;
the whole universe reflects your glory,
and we worship you.

Amen.

End the session by offering refreshments if that's what you've decided to do. Remind the group to bring their folders with them next week and to fill in their Personal Connections Sheets using the multi-choice questions if they can. Tell them that at the end of the course there will be an opportunity to see you individually if they want to talk about anything that might have arisen during the course.

TWO

PERSONAL CONNECTIONS SHEET

Genesis 1:1–2, 4

In the beginning, when God created the universe, the earth was formless and desolate. The raging ocean that covered everything was engulfed in total darkness, and the Spirit of God was moving over the water. God was pleased with what he saw. Then he separated the light from the darkness.

-- - fold here -- -

PERSONAL REFLECTIONS

CONNECTING VERSE

God is the one who made the mountains and created the winds. He makes his thoughts known to people; he changes day into night. He walks on the heights of the earth. This is his name; the Lord God Almighty!

Amos 4:13

The stories and their connections.

STORY CONNECTION

So what do you think God is like?
Here are some multi-choice questions to get you thinking:

In my life God has been:
a) always there
b) not very relevant when I had a problem
c) someone I remembered when I had a problem
d) someone I think about sometimes

If I had been Noah I would have:
a) not believed God when he told me that the whole world was going to flood
b) just got on with building the Ark in case
c) tried to tell everyone they were going to die unless they listened
d) tried asking God not to do it

In my experience God has been:
a) caring
b) tough
c) like a parent
d) like a friend

I want to live a good life because:
a) it's the right thing to do
b) it means things go better for you in the end
c) I love God
d) I don't want to hurt others

These questions are just to get you thinking. If you want to tick more than one answer, that's fine. Why not compare what you have chosen with others, or get the person leading your group to say what they would put and why? Or you could make up some multi-choice questions of your own.

Lord, how can we ever thank you enough
for all that you are,
for all that you have done?
We praise you for the wonder
of all that lives
and grows.
We praise you for pattern and order,
the complex and the simple.
The whole universe reflects your glory.
From the wideness of space,
to the detail of cells;
from the rainbow to the raindrop,
from the frog to the whale;
the whole universe reflects your glory,
the whole universe reflects your glory,
and we worship you.

Amen.

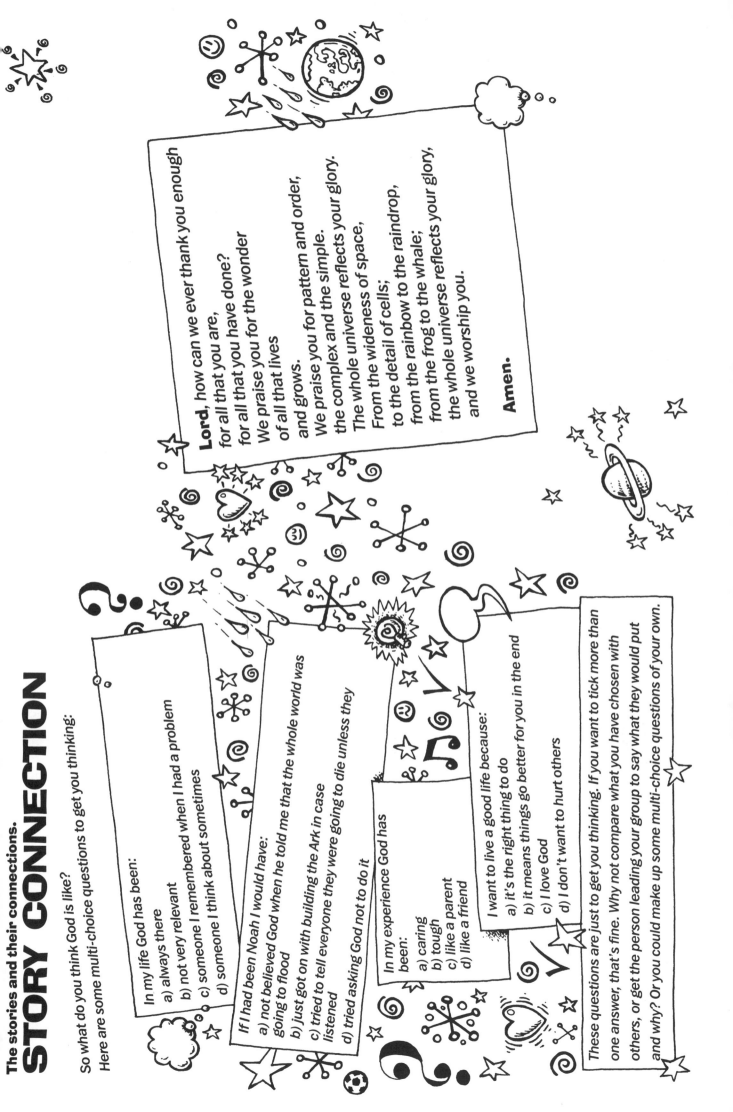

Connecting with God the Son

This session aims... to show how Jesus redeems us and opens the way for us into the presence of God.

Before the session starts... prepare yourself by reading the material you will be using in the session. Prayerfully read through the Bible passage.

Prepare the room you will be using for the session. Have ready pencils and the Personal Connections Sheets for each member of the group, plain A4 sheets of paper and spare Bibles. You'll also need an old sheet and some safety pins, some toy money, or foreign coins (or make up some fake £5.00 notes from scrap paper) and a dog lead, or a rope or chain. For the liturgy in the Concluding Connections you'll also need a cross, a small wooden one would be ideal, and a small candle.

First Connections

Welcome the group to this session. Answer any questions that may have arisen from the last session and ask about the multi-choice questions on the Personal Connections Sheets. Then briefly outline what you are going to be looking at this week.

Explain that you are going to play a game called the slavery game. Make a toga out of the old sheet and dress up one of the more confident members of the group. Explain that you are going to re-enact a slave market scene. Split the rest of the group into the following: a small group of sellers and a larger group of buyers. The sellers have to think of four positive attributes of the slave that would make him/her an attractive purchase. When they have done that, invite the sellers to make a sales pitch. Give the buyers varying amounts of money and start the bidding. You play the auctioneer. Allow the sellers first to make a short speech explaining why their slave is such a good buy. Then encourage the buyers to open the bidding. The winning buyer is given a dog lead, or chain to lead their slave back to their seat after the auction!

Encourage the group to say how they felt playing each part. Start with the slave. Was it a nice or nasty experience? What would a real slave auction be like? Although they had fun playing the game, what would it really feel like to be sold into slavery?

Ask the sellers how they felt. Was it easy to think of positive things to say about the slave? How did they feel about getting the money in return for the slave? Would they rather have money or a slave? What about the buyers, the unsuccessful ones first—they have got nothing! How do they feel? And the winner? How do they feel about having a slave? How might they treat their slave?

Make the point that slave auctions were a part of everyday life in New Testament times. Explain that the word 'redeemer' comes from that background. The word is derived from the practise of buying back something—often something that originally belonged to that person in the first place. Most often it refers to the buying of a slave in order to free him. The word comes from the same root as ransom.

Explain that the person playing the slave represents each one of us and the person who played the buyer represents Jesus. Go on to say that the reason why we are slaves in the first place is because of sin.

Bible Connections
Matthew 22:34–40

Sin is a difficult concept for young people to grasp. For young people from a church background it is often seen as lying, stealing, smoking, having sex before marriage—that kind of thing. For those who have little or no church background it is seen as a 'church' word that is totally irrelevant today, or they might see it as breaking the law—like burglary, or murder. Explain that, whilst there is truth in both these ways of looking at sin, it is in fact more that that. Sin is going our own way and not God's. It is the breaking of the great commandment which they will find in Matthew 22:34–40, 'Love the Lord your God with all your heart, with all your soul, and with all your mind... and love your neighbour as you love yourself...'

I have found that one of the best ways to explain sin to young people is through the parable of the prodigal son.

Further Connections

Explain that you are going to read from the Bible one of the stories which Jesus told. Remind the group that Jesus used stories to illustrate a point—to show his followers more of the truth about themselves and about the nature of God. Then settle back and read Luke 15:11–32.

When you have finished reading the story (or listening to your tape if you made one) your aim is to help the group make some connections between what they have just heard and their own lives, and to further that connection by exploring what Jesus, God's Son, might be saying to them as individuals.

Invite the group to start off by thinking themselves into the situation of the younger brother in the story. This exercise will help them to develop the skill of making theological links between the Bible and their own lives. It demonstrates how to read the Bible in a way that brings it alive and makes it relevant. This is one of the most important things that anybody who wants to be a Christian can learn. We need to be able to do this if we are to go forward in our journey of faith—for your group that will mean when they have finished this course and no longer have the group to support them (see the Conclusion on page 64). It is very important for all of us as Christians to develop the ability to do some of the thinking for ourselves.

Begin the meditation by setting the scene with the younger son. Recap how he grabbed hold of his father's money and went off. Think for a moment about what was happening to him. Why did he want the money? What sort of problems would he have caused his father by asking for it at this moment, rather than waiting until his father had died? It is probable that his father would have had to sell the farm in order to be able to divide the money, only retaining the management of the property. This would have been an unthought of situation in those days and Jesus doesn't give the details of what actually happened. However, the young man received the money he asked for and it soon became clear what he wanted to do with it: Spend! Spend! Spend! He set out to see the world. What would the group have done? Pause for a few moments to think about this and discuss it. Then continue with the story. The youngest son squandered his money, spending unwisely. Then two disasters struck him: he ran out of money just at the time when there was not enough food—a time of famine. The first disaster was his own fault, but not so the second. But isn't that just like life? Some things happen to us that are our own fault, but others occur over which we have little control. See if the group can parallel this in their own lives. For example, if they don't study for an exam and they fail then it is their fault, but if they were entered into an exam with a different syllabus by an ill-prepared teacher, then it is still a disaster, but they are not to blame. Can they think of other examples of similar things that have happened to them? Pause for a few moments to discuss this. Then continue with the meditation. The young man began to get worried and started to look for a job. He now had no family or friends around to help him. Does anyone in the group have a personal story of a time when they alienated themselves from family or friends by doing something from selfish motives which backfired? In our story the youngest son ended up tending pigs. Point out just how low that was for a Jewish boy and get the group to think of something today that would be as bad. A job that no one else would do—perhaps it might be helpful to think of the sort of jobs those on community service sentences have to do?

Continue with the story. The young man was hungry. Have any of the group ever been really hungry? It's unlikely that they have, but they may have been on a Duke of Edinburgh expedition and experienced hunger to some degree. The hardship brought the young man to his senses. Hardship often seems to cause people to face the facts in

life, doesn't it? The youngest son's motives for going home weren't the greatest—he was not particularly remorseful—he just wanted to be fed. The fact of the matter is that he wasn't sorry for what he had done, he was just sorry for what he had lost. That's true for us too. Often we are not very sorry for what we've done, just for what happened because of it. For example, we are not upset because we didn't revise, just that we didn't pass the exam. We are not sorry that we took the cream egg from the sweet shop, just that we were caught and now we look silly, and everyone knows.

Further Connections

 ## Connecting With God

What is true for the youngest son in Jesus' story is also true for us today, because sin causes us to be separated from God. We lose God, if you like. Like the young man in the story, we forfeit the right to call him Father; give up the right to be his children. But mostly people come to God, not because they are sorry for what they have done which caused the separation in the first place, but because they recognize that Christians have got something they haven't—for example, a peace about their lives and a sense of purpose in what they are doing. They might recognize this even before they know what God can give them—before they know anything at all about the relationship he offers them as their heavenly Father, or the friendship they can enjoy with his Son, or the guidance of his Holy Spirit. Ask the group if any of this makes sense to them, or reflects their own experience. Eventually the young man went back. Jesus tells us he went back to his father—not to the village, or his home—but to his father. I think that is significant. We must turn to God, not to the Church. In the confirmation service in the Anglican church the Bishop asks, 'Do you turn to Christ, do you renounce your sins?'. He doesn't ask if we want to join the Church.

In the story the father had been watching for his son's return and, when he saw him coming along

the road, he was filled with pity and ran towards him. Make the point here that as soon as we turn from our sins to face towards God again, he comes to meet us; he runs towards us. He greets us with much rejoicing. Ask if anyone in the group has had an experience like that? Perhaps they can remember a time when they had done something they knew to be wrong, had taken some steps to put it right, perhaps said sorry, and then experienced a feeling of relief and joy when they realized they were valued and accepted by the person they had wronged? In the father's welcome of his younger son Jesus teaches us that his heavenly Father welcomes those who return to him after going their own way; that going our own way is sin.

At this point we can turn to look at the reaction of the elder son. Here Jesus' teaching is for those who aren't tolerant of the returning sinner. The elder son is angry. He has always done all the right things and yet the party is for his brother. What do the group think about this? Do they know how he feels? Can they give examples from their own lives? Take a few minutes to discuss their experiences. However, the father loves both his sons equally and speaks with great kindness to the elder son. But when all is said and done he continues to throw the party, because his youngest son had been lost—he had cut himself off from the person who cared most about him, and now he has regained the relationship.

The Big Question

Explain that in order to help us to understand about the nature of God and the role that Jesus himself fulfilled, Jesus often told stories about everyday life, like this one about the lost son. The early Christians also used illustrations from everyday life to explain about Jesus. That's why they used the word 'redeemer' to explain what God did through Jesus. So, the crucial question for this session is:

If sin is going our own way, not God's, what has Jesus' death got to do with our being made friends again with God and accepted by him?

Having posed the question, explain that God can't stand sin because it is a rejection of him and of his perfect way for us. Because he is holy and perfect, we are all cut off from his presence. Sin comes between us and God like a thick fog. We have become so used to going our own way that we can't go God's any more. We have become slaves to doing only what we want, and it separates us from God. It would be helpful to tell a personal story at this point if you can. Because of the situation we are in, it is necessary for God to rescue us, to buy us back from the slavery we have got ourselves into, even if we don't realize it. Jesus, the Son of God, was without sin, but he was obedient to God, even to the point of giving up his life, and so paying the price for our turning away. Nothing else would have been good enough to clear away the fog. The price was for God to come to us as a human being and live a human life. The price was dying a criminal's death on a cross, with all our wrongdoings on his back—bearing the pain of our guilt. The result of Jesus' life and death is that he who redeemed us, the one who bought us back for himself, now owns us. Because of what Jesus was prepared to do for our sakes, he has opened the way for us to belong to God. In following Jesus we are able to experience the real freedom which was intended to be ours from the beginning of creation. When we connect with God through Jesus, we become our true selves in the way that God always intended us to be. We can come into his presence, friends at last with our Creator.

Concluding Connections

Explain that you are going to use a piece of liturgy to help the group to draw together all you have covered in this session and to bring it before God. Explain what a liturgy is: a written form of praise or prayer, mostly with responses, sometimes with different people reading different sections. A liturgy can take the form of a written service, or part of one. Point out that, although liturgies are most commonly found in prayer books—like those in the Church of England, written by Cranmer in 1662, and subsequently updated—they can in fact be written by anyone and can often play a special part in a service which the young people themselves might be putting together—a youth service in their own church, for example.

I have given a sample liturgy which I have used with groups, but if you don't want to use mine you could make one up of your own—or use a set liturgy, for example, 'The Drama of Incarnation' and 'The Drama of Salvation' from the *Iona Community Worship Book*, page 49, or 'Prayers at the Foot of the Cross' from *Celebrating Common Prayer*, page 271.

You can either sit or stand, as you feel most comfortable, as you pray the liturgy together.

1st reader: *We place this sheet here, as a sign, to help us remember that we were once slaves to sin.*
2nd reader: *When we were still far off God met us in his Son, Jesus, and brought us home.*
3rd reader: *We place this cross here, as a sign, to help us remember that Jesus died to pay the price for our sin.*
4th reader: *Do not be ashamed to belong to the faith of Christ crucified*
5th reader: *We place this light here, as a sign, to help us remember that we are now to live in the light, that we belong to God.*
All: *Help us to live as slaves for you, for that is real freedom.*

At the end of the session, as this is your third week together, it might be appropriate to ask the group if the course is working out as they expected. Is there anything that would make it more helpful for them? Be as open as you can to their suggestions, and feel free to adapt any of the course material to suit you and your group. You do not have to follow the course word for word, but feel free to use the ideas you find most helpful and add your own material as you see fit.

Personal Connections Sheet

Matthew 22:34-40

When the Pharisees heard that Jesus had silenced the Sadducees, they came together, and one of them, a teacher of the Law, tried to trap him with a question. 'Teacher,' he asked, 'which is the greatest commandment in the Law?' Jesus answered, ' "Love the Lord your God with all your heart, with all your soul, and with all your mind." This is the greatest and the most important commandment. The second most important is like it: "Love your neighbour as you love yourself." The whole Law of Moses and the teachings of the prophets depend on these two commandments.'

Three

Personal Reflections

Connecting Verse

Everyone has sinned and is far away from God's saving presence. But by the free gift of God's grace all are put right with him through Christ Jesus, who sets them free.   Romans 3: 23-24

1st Reader: We place this sheet here, as a sign, to help us remember that we were once slaves to sin.

2nd Reader: When we were still far off God met us in his Son, Jesus, and brought us home.

3rd Reader: We place this cross here, as a sign, to help us remember that Jesus died to pay the price for our sin.

4th Reader: Do not be ashamed to belong to the faith of Christ crucified.

5th Reader: We place this light here, as a sign, to help us remember that we are now to live in the light, that we belong to God.

All: Help us to live as slaves for you, for that is real freedom

---

In terms of what type of person you are—your personality—are you more like:

a) the son

b) the father

c) the older brother

Compared with the story, where are you with God:

a) at home, but not happy

b) in a far country away from God

c) coming to your senses

d) on your way home

e) just arrived

f) at the party

Write down some of your thoughts this week about sin. What do you think God would most want to change about your life? How do you think he wants to help you make that change?

Connecting with God the Holy Spirit

This session aims... to help the group explore together the idea of God as Trinity. It is designed to help your young people to be able to begin thinking on an individual basis of the Holy Spirit as the one who gives them life.

Before the session starts... prepare yourself by reading the material you will be using in the session. Prayerfully read through the Bible passage.

Prepare the room you will be using for the session. Have three large pieces of paper. On the first write FATHER, on the second write SON and on the third write HOLY SPIRIT. Collect together some pictures with images of the Holy Spirit on them. For example, pictures of doves, fire, wind and so on. Buy enough candles for each member of the group to have one each. Ordinary household candles will do. You need to tie them up with a ribbon, giving each one a bow to make it look like a present or gift. Have ready the Personal Connections Sheets.

First Connections

Welcome the group to this session. Answer any questions that may have arisen last time and briefly outline what you are going to be looking at in this session.

Have the room set up so that your three pieces of paper can be seen by all the group members. Explain that Christians believe in one God, but that they think of God in three ways: as Father, Son and Holy Spirit. Ask them if they can think of anything in everyday life which is one element, but exists in three states. The obvious example is water. Water can be ice, steam and liquid. It is the same in terms of its molecular structure, but it looks different and can do different things in its three states. Coffee could be another example, with the beans being one form, ground coffee ready to be put in a cafétière or percolator as the second and freeze-dried granules of instant coffee as the third. All three states are coffee, but all are different. I'm sure your group can think of other examples.

The Trinity was described to me in a very helpful way by a theological student from Wycliffe Hall in Oxford called Simon Walker who was on placement with me. He described it like this: the Father is like the mind—he is the planner who has the ideas, the creator side of God. Jesus is the Word—the part of God that is explicit, showing what God is thinking and what he is like. The Holy Spirit is like the breath on which the Word is carried. He is the means by which the Word comes to us. The Holy Spirit makes Jesus and the Father available to us, he is the means by which God is conveyed—God in action in his world.

Invite the group to write on the sheets of paper the things that they thought of which exist in three states: ice, steam, water; beans, grounds, granules; mind, word, breath and so on. Try to get them to think about which one fits naturally with each form of the Godhead. Is the Holy Spirit more like the coffee beans or the granules, and why? Remind them that in the last session you talked about how Jesus and the early Christians used everyday things around them to help them to understand God, and explain that that is what you are doing now. This skill is vital to all young Christians if they are to grow and develop once they are away from the group. It is important to be able to recognize God in the mundane things of everyday life, as well as in the special focus he is given in a church-orientated experience. This is theological thinking at its most creative. You will need to help them to check out what they come up with in the Bible, but let them be as creative as possible.

Be very encouraging with this exercise and, when you have completed it, put the sheets of paper in a place of prominence to convey the importance of what you are doing together.

Bible Connections
Romans 8:1–2, 6, 9–10, 14–15

We are going to use Romans 8 to increase our understanding of God's Holy Spirit. As the group leader you need to have read the whole chapter, but the group are only going to look at certain parts of it. You need to have the whole thing in your mind to ensure that you present as complete a picture as possible to your group.

Hand out the Personal Connections Sheets for this week which have the passages we are using printed on them.

Life in the Spirit
There is no condemnation now for those who live in union with Christ Jesus. For the law of the Spirit, which brings us life in union with Christ Jesus, has set me free from the law of sin and death... To be controlled by human nature results in death; to be controlled by the Spirit results in life and peace... But you do not live as your human nature tells you to; instead, you live as the Spirit tells you to—if, in fact, God's Spirit lives in you. Whoever does not have the Spirit of Christ does not belong to him. But if Christ lives in you, the Spirit is life for you, because you have been put right with God... Those who are led by God's Spirit are God's children. For the Spirit that God has given you does not make you slaves and cause you to be afraid; instead the Spirit makes you God's children.

Invite your group to read the passage through together, or read it through yourself—don't forget to use your cassette recording if you have made one. When you have finished reading the passage go on to explain that you are going to look at life in the Spirit in more depth, using the 'Swedish Symbol Sharing' method—honestly, that's what it's called!—from John Mallison's book *Growing Christians in Small Groups*, published by Scripture Union (used by permission).

You'll find the details in the Personal Connections Sheets. This is how it works:

Further Connections

First, appoint someone to read each allotted part of the passage. Then go on to explain what each symbol on their sheet means. The light bulb stands for something that you never realized before, that sheds light on something for you. The question mark stands for something you do not understand, or puzzles you. And the arrow stands for something that strikes you personally, that seems relevant to you.

Ask the person chosen to read the first part of the passage to read their section slowly. Then give the group a few minutes to fill out the sheet.

Allow enough time for them to write something in each box. Now encourage the group to share what they have written—it is usually best to start with the light bulb and for you as leader to go first. When you have looked at the first section of the passage in this way, go on to study the rest of the Bible reading in a similar fashion. This kind of study, which is more demanding of the group, would probably be far too threatening for a new group, but by doing it at this stage, having gained their confidence by showing them that you are willing to tell them personal stories, it can be a very rewarding method of study. It is very important that you take the time to make sure that you are very familiar with the whole passage yourself. If possible have some commentaries and books that might be of help with any questions raised. Once again, be prepared to research further, or find someone who can answer the questions that you cannot answer yourself so that you can bring the answers back to the group next time.

Dealing with the question marks is quite a skill, but try not to get bogged down with deep concepts—the aim of the session is for the group to get an insight into who the Holy Spirit is.

Connecting With God

When you have finished the exercise, you need to summarize the results, recapping on what has been difficult to understand and what has been particularly relevant. Discuss your summary under the following headings:

- *The Holy Spirit is the Spirit of God.*

- *As Christians we have God's Holy Spirit in us.*

- *Having God's Holy Spirit in us causes us to lead different lives.*

- *When we are led by the Holy Spirit we become God's children.*

- *The Holy Spirit makes our lives fruitful (turn to Galatians 5:22–23 to discuss this further).*

- *The Holy Spirit brings Life, with a capital 'L'. Not only does he make our lives fruitful, he also brings new life. Where there was death, it is God's Holy Spirit who brings things into being. (Turn to Genesis 1:1 to remind your group of the Spirit's presence at the beginning of creation.)*

The Big Question

Move on to explore the big question for this session:

What difference does the Holy Spirit make inside me personally?

Give the group time to think about the question, encouraging them to look at it in the light of the previous exercise and discussions. Then kick off further discussion by sharing with them ways in which the Holy Spirit has made a difference to you personally. Will what God has been saying to you in this session lead you to act or think in a different way? It is very important that the young people see you relating the Bible to your own life—this is how they will learn that Bible study has to be personal. Explain to them that Bible study is not like homework—something they do in order to absorb information. Instead the Bible is a vibrant 'living' document which will help them to live their lives. As Christians we never stop learning about God and we never stop listening to what he has to say to us. Often the Bible is the means he uses to do this.

Concluding Connections

Have ready some of the pictures you have collected which symbolize the Holy Spirit. You can make quite a good collection—perhaps by going through recent Sunday supplements. Look in card shops for photographic style cards that might be suitable. Poster shops and cut-price bookshops can also be a help. Christian bookshops often have posters—or rescue some old ones from the church hall (cut off any words if you can). Covers of books about the Holy Spirit may help, coffee table type books from the local library might be a possibility, as might a local photographic club, or your church's 'arty' person. Just select a few of those you feel are most appropriate. Set the pictures out and explain that in a time of quiet you are going to ask the group to think about the Holy Spirit. Ask them to think silently about which image they like and why. Is there one image that they feel is like the Spirit inside them? Have they had a time when they felt that God's Holy Spirit was operating like a dove, or fire, for example—in them, or in a situation, or another person? Now, quietly pass out pens, put some music on and explain that in the quiet you want them to write a poem about how they see the Holy Spirit in relation to themselves. There is space in their Personal Connections Sheets for them to do this. It can be as simple as they like, as personal or as impersonal, and they won't have to show anyone if they don't want to. The aim is for them to be able to make the connection with God the Holy Spirit by experiencing the theory of God as Spirit as a personal reality. They will be used to writing poems at school, so you do not need to worry about asking them to do this exercise. They will be far less inhibited than a group of adults would be if you asked them to do the same thing. By writing something down you are encouraging them to interact with what you have been discussing about God's Spirit. By enabling them to do this themselves you are demonstrating how to take what they have learnt and relate it to their lives. They change from being consumers of God's kingdom to being co-creators in it. It's yet another ingredient in the mix that will empower them to go forward on their spiritual journey.

When they have finished writing their poems, ask if anyone is prepared to read out their poem aloud to the group and, if they are, allow them to read without comment. If no one volunteers you can use some from a group that I have just had the privilege to lead. The writers of these poems have agreed to their being used. Their poems are on the Personal Connections Sheets.

When you have finished reading the poems, give out the candles tied with ribbon, explaining that they represent the gift of the Holy Spirit available to all Christians, freely given by God—his gift of Life. Explain that we constantly need 'topping up', as it were, with God's Spirit and say that you are giving these candles to them as a sign that God gives us his Holy Spirit as a gift. When they untie the gift bow and light the candle it will be a reminder to them that God wants to rekindle his flame in us, by the gift of his Spirit, every day anew. Explain that they are a present from you for them to use in their quiet times with God. Once again you are encouraging them to see their Christian life as a full time commitment—not just something that they think about here at the group or in church on Sunday. You are conveying the idea to them that as Christians they need to have times of quiet with God every day.

Encourage them, if they can over the coming week, to try to remember their poem. Finish the session by explaining that in the next session you are going to be looking at what it means to be a Christian in everyday life—not just when in church and with Christian friends. Suggest to them that they might like to report back when you next meet on any ways in which they have thought that the Holy Spirit has helped them.

Four

PERSONAL CONNECTION SHEET

Romans 8:1–2, 6, 9–10, 14–15

Life in the Spirit

There is no condemnation now for those who live in union with Christ Jesus. For the law of the Spirit, which brings us life in union with Christ Jesus, has set me free from the law of sin and death... To be controlled by human nature results in death; to be controlled by the Spirit results in life and peace... But you do not live as your human nature tells you to; instead, you live as the Spirit tells you to—if, in fact, God's Spirit lives in you. Whoever does not have the Spirit of Christ does not belong to him. But if Christ lives in you, the Spirit is life for you because you have been put right with God... Those who are led by God's Spirit are God's children. For the Spirit that God has given you does not make you slaves and cause you to be afraid; instead the Spirit makes you God's children.

---

fold here

PERSONAL REFLECTIONS

Over the week you can use this space to record your thoughts and feelings about the Holy Spirit. You might like to think about how the Holy Spirit has helped you. What does this help feel like and what form does it take?

CONNECTING VERSE

We have not received this world's spirit; instead, we have received the Spirit sent by God, so that we may know all that God has given us.

1 Corinthians 2:12

The Swedish Symbol Sharing Method

Help us
Omnipotent,
Loving,
Young for ever.
Show us your true way,
Power over all,
Intelligence,
Righteousness,
Inspiration,
Telepathic.

Michael

As a baby I was baptised into the Holy Spirit
family,
accepted by him into the flock.
To grow,
to know
him more.
Knowing he is by my side
gives me the strength to survive.
Going to his house to join in praise and song
is what helps me along.
Growing up and getting older means I'm
more into his family,
the understanding's deeper,
the Holy Spirit is with me.

Jenny

SYMBOL	VERSE	COMMENT
Sheds light on something		
Something you do not understand		
Something that strikes you as relevant for you		

Connecting with God the Father

This session aims... to show how being a Christian doesn't happen in isolation. It is about being in community in our Christian family, with God as our Father, and requires us to take responsibility for others.

Before the session starts... prepare yourself by reading the material you will be using in the session. Prayerfully read through the Bible passage.

Prepare the room you will be using for the session. Have ready pencils and the session's Personal Connections Sheets for each member of the group, plain A4 sheets of paper and spare Bibles. You'll also need five large sheets of plain paper and an old phone book that can be ripped up!

First Connections

Welcome the group to this session. Answer any questions that may have arisen last time and briefly outline what you are going to be looking at in this session.

Begin the session by performing the classic 'tearing a phone book in half' trick.

Explain that you are going to rip a phone book in half, only, not being very strong, you are going to give in and reveal the secret of how it is done. Explain that if you try to rip the phone book conventionally you have to be very strong and, as you are not, the trick is to fan out the pages and to rip slowly. Then actually what you are doing is ripping each page one at a time in very quick succession. This is perfectly possible and it looks as if you are amazingly strong!

Let the group have a go and see how well they can make the trick work. When you have had enough fun, explain to them that this is what being part of the family of God is about. A single page of paper can easily be ripped, but when you put the pages together they become much stronger—the sum of the parts is stronger than the individual pieces. This is how the family of God works. God is our heavenly Father (or the person who cares about us more than any other) and we are his children—that includes everyone who is a Christian, the members of our church, those in other churches, Christians all over the world, together with Christians who have died—we are all part of the family of God, God's community, his 'body'. We are all part of a massive phone directory—the Book of Life!

There has been a lot of emphasis in recent times on personal spirituality—on making a personal decision and having a personal relationship with God. All this is valid and necessary, but as Christians we are called to live in community with others to gain strength from one another and to bear one another's burdens. In this session we are going to look at what it means for us to be part of the family of which God is the Father—part of the flock of which Jesus is the shepherd. We are going to explore the lessons each of us can learn about being part of God's family—about the way we are to treat each other and what it might mean for us as Christians in a society which teaches that the rights of the individual come before anything else.

Bible Connections

Luke 12:22–34

The Bible passage I have chosen for this session may not strike you immediately as an obvious choice, but hopefully it will become clear! Sometimes Jesus talks to us about God being a very loving Father, and, although it is good to realize that we are part of his family, it's not always easy to relate positively to the picture of a Father. At other times Jesus talks about a shepherd and about the care and love the shepherd has for his flock. This is a good picture of God's care for his family and is very helpful for those who haven't been able to experience the care of a good father in their own family situation. Don't forget to choose the way of presenting the passage which best suits your group—either with you reading it, members of your group reading it, or using a pre-recorded tape. With this particular passage, I have found it useful to use the appropriate section of the video, *Jesus of Nazareth*. This or another video of Christ's life may provide you with a fresh approach to the reading which will help you to maintain an element of interest in the way that you present the Bible passage.

Having read the passage you need to develop the following points:

• *Jesus commands us not to worry. He doesn't advise us, he tells us. Worry is an inhibitor to life, it stops you from doing things. When we live in a constant state of anxiety we miss out on what life's really all about.*

• *We are not to be like the pagans—people who don't know God—we must live differently.*

• *We are to be positive. Together we must seek God's kingdom, not sit around waiting for his kingdom to come to us.*

• *We are the 'little flock' to whom God, our loving heavenly Father, will give the kingdom. In our weakness God our Father and Jesus our Shepherd will provide.*

There are two ways to approach this study. You can either just lead a discussion on the passage, focusing on the above points and making sure all the verses are covered, or, if your group is less suited to this technique, then a differently structured approach may help. I suggest using an 'application' method of Bible study, which has helped me with the groups I have worked with.

With the 'application' method there are five questions to be answered which will help you to apply the study to life. The questions are on the Personal Connections Sheets for this session. They are:

1. Is there a command to obey?

2. Is there anything in my life which isn't right and which I must stop or guard against?

3. Is there a promise that I can claim? Does it have any conditions?

4. Is there an example to follow?

5. Is there a new truth which God is showing me, or my community?

Split your group into smaller cells of two or three to answer the questions and then gather back to share the answers. Appoint a scribe from each group to write up the group's answers to each question on large sheets of paper. This can help concentration and participation. With the groups I work with I have found it useful to write each of the questions on top of separate sheets of paper and then pass the sheets around to each smaller cell, inviting them to take it in turns to fill in their answers and then pass the sheet on to the next cell and so on. This seems to work quite well. When all the questions have been answered by each cell, you can then look at the answers together. However you choose to organize the exercise, the aim is, of course, to encourage the group to study the passage in some depth in order to stimulate thought and increase understanding.

Further Connections

I love the contrast in verse 32 of this passage: 'Do not be afraid, little flock, for your Father is pleased to give you the Kingdom.' Weakness and strength, a flock and a kingdom! You are a little flock says Jesus. It's a form of address that is used nowhere else in the New Testament. It conveys how few the numbers of true disciples are and how vulnerable to wolves—and yet it also speaks to us of how caring our shepherd is and how loving our Father.

Young people, especially those who have grown up in an urban or inner city environment, will not find analogies with shepherds particularly helpful, but I'm sure if you ask them about their experiences of trying to be a Christian at school they will express

feelings of vulnerability—like a little flock of sheep. Jesus says that in that very weakness and dependence on him lies our strength, because we are inheritors of the kingdom. Jesus then goes on directly to talk about God's gift of the kingdom for us—not a gift that has to be wrung from him unwillingly, but his precious gift to us, willingly given. Jesus tells us that our Father God longs to give us freely that very thing we have been told to seek. How do we seek his kingdom? By behaving in the way we know we should, by trying to produce in our lives the kind of conduct appropriate to someone who is a child of God, and by telling others about God's ways, so the kingdom grows. We are the little flock, the family of God whose job it is to seek the kingdom. We are to live our lives simply, helping those in need, being good neighbours, and concentrating our energies together on the growth of God's kingdom.

Connecting With God

It would be good at this point to talk to your group about what it feels like for them to be a Christian in their community. Do they feel like just one page of that phone book—a small, isolated, easily torn individual—or do they feel part of the family of God?

If they feel confident as Christians, is it because of a Christian Union, or because their friends are Christians, or is it something else? If they feel weak is it because they are not part of a Christian family or community? It may be that they are partly

responsible for how they feel—perhaps they have spent time building up treasure in the wrong places—or it may be that their church fellowship and family have not considered how they may need to be supported in order to feel part of that family. Get the group to carry out a small survey about their church life and to what extent they feel part of the church family on a day-to-day basis. You'll find the outline for the survey on the Personal Connections Sheets for this session. When they have completed the survey take a few minutes to discuss the results and then fill out the last section. What would have to change to make the crosses move up the lines?

The Big Question

You have now reached the point where the crucial question can be posed. This week the question is easy to ask, but not at all easy to answer:

What would you have to do to feel more of a part of God's family?

This is a hard question to answer because most people immediately take the approach of thinking in terms of what others should do in order to make *them* feel part of the family. That undoubtedly is a valid question. However, the question also needs to be approached from the opposite angle: 'What can

I do to make others feel more a part of the family? Now, the young people in your group are unlikely to be able to do very much to change the attitudes and actions of other people in their church, but they can change their own. If you sense that your discussion is indicating a strong feeling in your group that the church family is not at all supportive, then it may be appropriate for you to offer to feed back some of their comments to the church leadership and to look together at ways in which the situation can be improved.

Concluding Connections

Families are about sharing things together, about support in good times and bad. Explain to the group that you would like to draw the session together in the presence of God by using some words from the marriage ceremony that have been specially adapted for the family of God to say to each other. Remind them of verse 30 of the passage from Luke you have been studying before you say the words together—that, as members of his family, God knows what we need.

I, (name) accept the family of God,
known and unknown, to be my family...
for better, for worse,
for richer, for poorer,
in sickness and in health,
to love and to cherish,
till death, when I'll just continue in heaven.
In the name of God, Father, Son and Holy Spirit.

Amen.

Go through the words with the group slowly, asking them to think of examples of people in God's family that they know or have heard of that fit each of the categories. For example, for richer: our group almost all thought of a family in our church with a large house with a swimming pool, or one of our congregation who owns a successful accountancy practice. For poorer: they thought of our link church of Christ Church in Nazareth and some young people they had met from there who seemed to have almost no possessions. In sickness: they all knew someone from our church who has been in hospital for a long period of time.

When they have got someone or several people in mind for each category then say the words out aloud together. Remind them that they are saying them to God, their heavenly Father, and that the words form a prayer. They need to think seriously about the words. If they feel they can't say them, it might be best for them to listen quietly while the rest of the group says them together. In this way, those who are unsure can feel part of the whole. You can either stand or sit together as you say the prayer, each person putting his or her name in the space.

Finish the session by providing refreshments if that is what you have decided to do and give a good positive send-off and warm invitation to the next session. Don't forget to feed back anything that came out of the session to your minister if appropriate. You'll be showing your group that you really care if you can give constructive answers to their practical questions as well as their theological ones!

PERSONAL CONNECTIONS SHEET

Luke 12:22-34

Then Jesus said to the disciples, 'And so I tell you not to worry about the food you eat to stay alive or about the clothes you need for your body. Life is much more important than food, and the body much more important than clothes. Look at the crows: they don't sow seeds or gather a harvest; they don't have store-rooms or barns; God feeds them! You are worth so much more than birds! Can any of you live a bit longer by worrying about it? If you can't manage even such a small thing, why worry about the other things?

Look how the wild flowers grow: they don't work or make clothes for themselves. But I tell you that not even King Solomon with all his wealth has clothes as beautiful as one of these flowers. It is God who clothes the wild grass—grass that is here today and gone tomorrow, burnt up in the oven. Won't he be all the more sure to clothe you? How little faith you have!

So don't be all upset, always concerned about what you will eat and drink. (For the pagans of this world are always concerned about all these things.) Your Father knows that you need these things. Instead, be concerned with his Kingdom, and he will provide you with these things.

1) Is there a command to obey?
2) Is there anything in my life which isn't right and which I must stop or guard against?
3) Is there a promise that I can claim? Does it have any conditions?
4) Is there an example to follow?
5) Is there a new truth which God is showing me or my community?

Five

PERSONAL REFLECTIONS

Record your thoughts about how you feel about being a member of God's family. Do you like the other members? What might God want you to do to be more a member of his family?

CONNECTING VERSE

If you have love for one another, then everyone will know that you are my disciples.

John 13:35

fold

Church life survey

1) Who is the person you know best at church? (Not a member of your family.)

2) Does this person know you?:
   a) very well
   b) quite well
   c) not very well
   d) hardly at all

3) Do you go to church?
   a) because you like the people who go
   b) because God wants you to
   c) because you have to please your family
   d) because you want to

4) Do you think anyone at church prays for you?

5) Do you see any members of your church during the week? Who are they and when do you see them?

6) If the church is a family, who in your church acts like a parent, who like a grandparent, and who like a brother or sister?

7) Do you feel part of a family at your church? Do you feel loved and valued, and expected to do your share of the 'housework'?

8) Mark on the line on the page opposite where you feel you are. One end is being a full member of the family of your church and the other is being an outsider.

I, (your name) accept the family of God, known and unknown, to be my family...
for better, for worse,
for richer, for poorer,
in sickness and in health,
to love and to cherish,
till death, when I'll just continue in heaven.
In the name of God, Father, Son and Holy Spirit.

Amen.

outsider

full member

Session Six

Connecting with the Bible

This session aims... to encourage the group to see the Bible as a tool in their spiritual lives that can help them be more Christ-like and to help them learn more about what it means to open their lives and hearts to God's word.

Before the session starts... prepare yourself by reading the material you will be using in the session. Prayerfully read through the Bible passage.

Prepare the room you will be using for the session. Have ready pencils and the session's Personal Connections Sheets for each member of the group, plain A4 sheets of paper and spare Bibles. You'll also need some blindfolds.

First Connections

Welcome the group to this session. Answer any questions that may have arisen last time and briefly outline what you are going to be looking at in this session.

This session starts with a blindfold walk. You need to have put some thought in beforehand as to where would be the best place to take the group. It could be indoors—a circular route, including some stairs, narrow doors etc. Going under a rope previously laid between two chairs, or negotiating a short obstacle course would be fun. Or perhaps you might feel it's better to be out-of-doors. The last group I did this with used a route around the estate on which we live. It's fairly quiet and, being outside, seemed to work rather well. Use your own judgment to pick the options and scale of difficulty that you think will challenge your group, but not be dangerous or frightening for them. Arrange the group in pairs. It is probably best to partner them with someone they know fairly well. Explain that in their pairs they are going for a short walk, but it will be a walk with a slight difference in that one person in each pair will be blindfolded! Allow them time to decide between themselves who will be the one to be blindfolded. Make sure that you are sensitive to the fact that some young people can be very scared if they can't see and make sure no one is forced to do anything they don't want to do. Take the unblindfolded partners to one side and explain the route to them. Point out to them that their partner will be depending on them to guide them safely. Impress upon them the responsibility of this and ask them to be as sensitive as possible, telling them not to guide by pushing and shoving, but by quietly giving accurate instructions. Now blindfold those who have opted to be led, explaining that their partners are going to guide them by their voices, watching all the time to check their safety.

When the walk is over, invite the group to sit back down and, as a group, talk about what you've just done using the following points to spark your discussion:

• Walking through life sometimes feels as if you can't see where you are going—none of us really knows what is going to happen next. The future is not revealed to us, we just walk into it not knowing what it will hold. That can be scary when we think about it, just as walking with a blindfold on is scary.

• Those who were blindfolded would not have fared very well if they had just been left to find their own way. When you can't see, things seem very different.

Bible Connections
Matthew 7:24–27

The guidance given by the partner not wearing the blindfold was vital in helping those who were blindfolded to negotiate the course. As Christians we have the Bible as our main source of guidance. If those who had been blindfolded had tried to walk without help it is more than likely that they would have fallen, or crashed into something—someone needed to interpret the terrain for them. The unblindfolded partners needed to say, 'There's a step coming up now,' or, 'Put your hand out and you'll feel the edge of the door,' and so on. The Bible is like that. It helps us to interpret things as God sees them. Of course, things aren't that simple. Discuss some of the mishaps that happened to the group. Did anyone fall over, or bump their head? If so what were the reasons? Was it because the instructions weren't clear, or was it that the hearer wasn't concentrating? Try to get the group to make parallels between their experiences on the walk and the Bible. For example, sometimes the Bible's message doesn't seem very clear to our modern ears—it might have been clear to those who heard its message when it was written, but as it wasn't originally written in English, the translation is sometimes difficult for us to understand. Encourage the group to voice some of the difficulties that they might have experienced personally with the Bible and discuss ways in which these difficulties might be overcome. You might need to give some examples yourself if your group does not have a good awareness of what the Bible contains.

The Bible passage that we are using for this session is Matthew 7:24–27, the parable of the two builders.

Before looking at the Bible passage with your group you need first to explain that the Bible, written over a period of more than 1,000 years and by many people from vastly differing backgrounds, is inevitably made up of different *types* of writing. Invite the group to suggest some of the types of writing that might be found in the Bible: poetry, story, historical accounts, letters and so on. To help your understanding of any given passage you need simply to ask four questions:

1. Who was this passage written for?

2. Who wrote it?

3. What did it mean to the people for whom it was written?

4. What does it mean to me and what do I think about it?

These questions are key to our faith development. Impress upon your group that they need to ask themselves these questions whenever they read the Bible. The Bible is not a dry document written by great scholars who have all the meanings worked out. Throughout history people have found that the Bible is able to speak into their own personal situation, because God's word is living and vibrant, speaking to each of us today as individuals.

Go on to give a practical demonstration of how we can use the four questions to help our understanding of a passage by using the story of the two house builders from Matthew's Gospel. Read the passage in whichever way you have chosen for this session and then discuss it in the light of the four questions.

Further Connections

As you explore the passage in more depth, don't just look at the answers to the questions but at what this passage might have to say about how we build our lives.

1. Who was this passage written for?
Here Matthew records the words of Jesus to the crowd. Jesus was talking to ordinary people, not particularly clever people, or religious people, or very bad people—just normal folk. Matthew was Jewish and wrote his Gospel for the Jewish people. He wanted them to believe that Jesus was the longed-for Messiah, so he particularly shows how Jesus is the fulfilment of all the Old Testament prophecies about the Messiah.

2. Who wrote it?
It is widely believed that this Gospel is written by the apostle Matthew. Matthew, which means incidentally, 'gift of the Lord', is sometimes called 'Levi'. As a tax collector, he was one of a hated

breed, shunned by his fellow countrymen. But, when Jesus called him, he left his old life behind to follow him. He must have loved Jesus very much, following him throughout his ministry, through the crucifixion to the resurrection and beyond. It is highly likely that Matthew was an eye witness to the events he recorded.

3. What did it mean to the people for whom it was written?

For the people Matthew was writing to, and for the people who first heard Jesus tell this story, its meaning must have been fairly clear: obey Jesus' words and you will stand up to the inevitable storms that life brings. What amazed his original hearers was the way Jesus spoke with such authority. He didn't say, 'Obey the Ten Commandments', he said, 'Obey MY words.'

4. What does it mean to me and what do I think about it?

At this point invite the group to answer the question themselves. Encourage them to apply the passage to their own lives and to discover for themselves what the Bible might be saying to them and their situations. Help them to make connections

between the Bible and themselves.

Here are some starter questions to help them focus their thoughts:

- *What, if anything, does the passage say about the Bible?*

- *What do you think Jesus means when he asks us to hear his words?*

- *What difference is there in reading about God in the Bible and hearing Jesus' words?*

- *What does Jesus say about the difference this will make to our lives?*

- *Why is it important to make Bible study a part of our lives?*

Point out that the storm comes to both the wise and the foolish builder. Listening and obeying Jesus doesn't make us immune to the storms, but it helps us deal with them.

- *Jesus says that building our lives on the word of God is the only thing that can bring stability. What do you think?*

Further Connections

Connecting With God

On the Personal Connections Sheet for this session there is a life graph, spanning life from the age of 3 to the age of 80. The aim of the exercise is to get the group to use their imaginations: what are their Bible reading habits likely to be over their lifetime and what factors will influence it? They need to mark their thoughts on the graph. For example, if they were to have a high-powered job at the age of 30

would their Bible reading drop to 'once a month'? Similarly, if their best friend died when they were 50, causing them to want to look for meaning to life, would their Bible reading go up to 'more than once a day'? Although this is an imaginary exercise, it is designed to highlight the difficulties we might encounter in reading the Bible as we go through life. Invite the group to do the exercise individually and then draw the group together at the end to compare their thoughts. Try to explore together suggestions which will help overcome the difficulties, using the passage to throw light on the answers to the questions that are raised.

The Big Question

The crucial question for this session is this:

How much of a commitment are you willing to make to reading your Bible regularly?

Jesus wants us to recognize the fact that the Bible must be given a central place in our lives if we are to grow as Christians. It's not so much about how often we read it, as about how important we see it as being. There is a pledge on the Personal Connections Sheet for each person to sign if they are ready to show their commitment to reading the Bible.

Concluding Connections

An appropriate way to end this session might be to use the liturgy below to help the group to think about why the Bible is God's 'living book'. I suggest that you invite a few members of the group to read each part of the liturgy and allow everyone to join in the responses. Make sure they know that they only need to join in if they feel they want to.

Place the group around a focal point and make sure they are comfortable; you might like to have a candle and a copy of the Bible as a focus. I find that using a low coffee table in a living room setting works well. Lowering the lights slightly and providing low background music also helps create a more contemplative atmosphere. Encourage the readers to read slowly and contemplatively too if you can!

Reader 1
Lord Jesus, it's good to know
that you lived as a human being,
walked where we walk, felt what we feel,
got tired, had sore and dirty feet,
needed to eat, and to think about
where the next meal was coming from.

Thank you for the record of your life, the Bible.

Reader 2
It's even better to know
that you enjoyed your food,
the feel of perfume on your skin,
the wind on your face, a child in your arms
and the good wine at the wedding.

Thank you for the record of your life, the Bible.

Reader 3
You didn't mind when people touched you,
even those who were thought to be unclean.
You kissed people with diseases
and laid your head on your friend's shoulder.

Thank you for the record of your life, the Bible.

Reader 4
Lord Jesus, it's good to know
that you studied the scripture too,
that you allowed it to shape your life,
as you designed it to shape ours.
That the laws in it are your laws
and the love in it your love.

Thank you for the record of your life, the Bible.
Amen.

This prayer is based on *The Pattern of our Days*, edited by Kathy Galloway, from the Wild Goose Resource Group of the Iona Community, Glasgow. Copyright © WGRG, Iona Community, Pearce Institute, 840 Govan Rd., Glasgow G51 3UU, Scotland. (Adapted).

Finish the session by providing refreshments if that's what you've decided to do. Check with the group that they have their own Bibles in a version they can understand. I have often found it necessary to buy Bibles for young people in my groups—they are often too expensive for a young person's pocket! The Bible is an essential part of our growth as Christians, so they won't be able to do without one!

Six

PERSONAL CONNECTIONS SHEET

Matthew 7:24–27

'So then, anyone who hears these words of mine and obeys them is like a wise man who built his house on rock. The rain poured down, the rivers overflowed, and the wind blew hard against that house. But it did not fall, because it was built on rock. But anyone who hears these words of mine and does not obey them is like a foolish man who built his house on sand. The rain poured down, the rivers overflowed, the wind blew hard against that house, and it fell. And what a terrible fall that was!'

1) Who was the passage written for?
2) Who wrote it?
3) What did it mean to the people for whom it was written?
4) What does it mean to me and what do I think about it?

- - - fold - - -

PERSONAL REFLECTIONS

Why is reading the Bible sometimes hard? Think of three reasons you would give to stop yourself feeling bad about not reading your Bible. Now think of three things which would answer your excuses.

Write down your feelings about trying to read the Bible. In what ways has it made a difference to your life?

PLEDGE

I, _____, promise to God to make the Bible my manual for life.

Signed _____

CONNECTING VERSE

All Scripture is inspired by God and is useful for teaching the truth, rebuking error, correcting faults, and giving instruction for right living, so that the person who serves God may be fully qualified and equipped to do every kind of good deed.

2 Timothy 3:16

Reader 1

Lord Jesus, it's good to know
that you lived as a human being,
walked where we walk, felt what we feel,
got tired, had sore and dirty feet,
needed to eat, and to think about
where the next meal was coming from.
Thank you for the record of your life, the Bible.

Reader 2

It's even better to know
that you enjoyed your food,
the feel of perfume on your skin,
the wind on your face, a child in your arms
and the good wine at the wedding.
Thank you for the record of your life, the Bible.

Reader 3

You didn't mind when people touched you,
even those who were thought to be unclean.
You kissed people with diseases
and laid your head on your friend's shoulder.
Thank you for the record of your life, the Bible.

Reader 4

Lord Jesus, it's good to know
that you studied the scripture too,
that you allowed it to shape your life,
as you designed it to shape ours.
That the laws in it are your laws
and the love in it your love.
Thank you for the record of your life, the Bible.
Amen.

based on a prayer from *The Pattern of Our Days* from the Wild
Goose Resource Group of the Iona Community in Glasgow

LIFE GRAPH

more than once a day										
once a day										
about once a week										
about once a fortnight										
about once a month										
when I need to										
a few times a year										
hardly ever										
never										
age	3	6	9	12	16	18	21	30	35	40 50 60 70 80

Connecting with Prayer

This session aims... to help the group to develop their understanding of prayer and to work out some strategies for building prayer into the pattern of everyday life.

Before the session starts... prepare yourself by reading the material you will be using in the session. Prayerfully read through the Bible passage.

Prepare the room you will be using for the session. Have ready pencils and the session's

Personal Connections Sheets for each member of the group, plain A4 sheets of paper and spare Bibles. You'll also need a selection of the collages you did in Session Two (they should be in the folders), two large sheets of plain paper, some scissors, and an envelope and a coloured feather (purchased from an art shop) for each member of the group.

First Connections

Welcome the group to this session. Answer any questions that may have arisen last time and briefly outline what you are going to be looking at in this session.

Prayer is a very big topic. To introduce it to your group you need to use a simple way of explaining the concept. The concept of conversation is an excellent illustration. I have found that young people from a church background relate to this concept very well indeed. Those from a non-church background tend to think of prayer as asking God for things. Prayer is, of course, both these things and this session aims to expand the group's understanding of prayer from these simple starting points.

Ease into the session by setting out some of the collages that the group made in Session Two. It doesn't matter if some of the group weren't there for that session, or if they didn't do a collage. Put all the collages where everyone can see them. Once more provide the stack of magazines that you used for creating the collages. Invite each member of the group to select one image which they feel represents Jesus and another to represent the Holy Spirit—they can cut out or tear their images from the magazines. Put all the images together on one

piece of paper, together with the selection of collages from Session Two. You now have a collection of images picturing the group's ideas about God. Point out how diverse they are. Are there any opposites, for example quiet pools and raging seas? Bright reds and cool blues? Now scatter the feathers over the pictures and point out that, just as a bird's feathers are an essential part of its being a bird and it cannot fly without them, so prayer is an essential part of our being a Christian and without it we cannot communicate with God. Go on to ask the question as to the ways we might communicate with the God portrayed in the images, and how might he communicate with us? Write up the group's ideas on a large sheet of paper.

Using these ideas, invite the group to create their own definition of prayer, for example, 'Prayer is being in communication with God.' Then go on to look at the ways in which:

1. God communicates with us.

2. We communicate with God.

Bible Connections

Luke 11:1–4

How are we supposed to pray? Jesus gave his followers an answer to this question and we'll use Luke 11:1–4 to see what that answer was. Read the passage out, or get someone you know likes to read aloud to read it (or use your tape if that is what you have decided to do).

Now turn back to the pictures. The group's task is to find an image which represents each word or phrase of the Lord's Prayer.

Father...
your holy name...
be honoured...
your kingdom come...
give us day by day the food we need...
forgive us our sins...

Further Connections

As the group picks an image for each part of the prayer, encourage them to discuss the meaning of the phrase together. There may well be quite a bit of discussion over words like 'honoured' for example. You may need to help the group to wrestle with some of the words so that their understanding is increased. The advantage of studying the Bible in this way is that the group learn without even noticing! And even if they can't find an image, for 'sins' for example, the work of finding out what we mean by sins will have been covered in searching for an image. As a point of interest the word 'honoured', or 'hallowed' in some translations, means 'holy' or 'reverenced'. A person's name in biblical times meant much more than it does for us today. It summed up a person's whole character, all that was known about them. Therefore, this prayer of Jesus concerns much more than merely the way

people say the name of God with their lips; it's about how we connect with God in our lives; about all that God is and how he has made himself known to us. We need to acknowledge this fact with a rightful attitude of reverence. The point is not that God should make his name holy, but that we should rightly honour him because of who and what he is. Similarly, the meaning of forgiveness of sins is linked to our ability to forgive others, in the knowledge of the deep truth that forgiveness comes from the grace of God, not by human merit. The concept behind the words is that if even we sinful humans can forgive how much more will our sinless God forgive us!

Connecting With God

Once the group have completed the exercise, you need to help them to apply their findings to their own lives. How is the advice that Jesus gave to his followers thousands of years ago going to help them make the connection with their Creator God today? Explain that you are going to try to come up with a list of six 'how to's for prayer, so that if someone asked them how to pray they would be able to give a clear answer. Explain that you are going to use the words of Jesus to help you to devise the list. Then ask the question, 'What exactly did Jesus ask us to do?' Well, he said that we should 'say' some words. So that's a good place to start.

Here's a suggested list you might come up with:

1. Speak to God

2. Use his name

3. Honour his name

4. Pray for his kingdom

5. Pray for forgiveness

6. Pray for his presence

When you have decided on your list you can fill in the 'How to pray' section on the Personal Connections Sheets.

The Big Question

The question in this session is a challenge to us all. Here it is:

Having decided on your list, will you use it as a foundation for daily prayer?

This question is a difficult one to answer as a group. On the Personal Connections Sheets you'll find a personal reflection section to help each group member to think through their own response. There has been much study on personality types and prayer (for example *Knowing Me, Knowing God* by Malcolm Goldsmith, published by Triangle), and these studies tend to show that different individuals will have a prayer style that suits their personality. Therefore those who are naturally contemplative should not be expected to sing loud worship songs in their time of private prayer if they are not comfortable doing so and, in the same way, extroverts should not have to sit still for hours meditating on one phrase from a Psalm. This seems to be fairly obvious—we are each unique, with our own unique ways of communicating with our God. However, there is a place in a busy life for stillness before God, even for extroverts, and there is a place for exuberant praise, even for the introvert. With this in mind, encourage discussion about the individual answers if your group are willing to share their thoughts. It is worthwhile to make the point that sometimes we don't feel like praying, but we should get into the habit of praying regularly, however we might feel.

Concluding Connections

When I was testing the material in this book with my group, the Concluding Connections to this session were very real and touched very deep places in all of us in the group. It may have been that the timing was right for the group, or that the setting was perfect, but, whatever the reasons, I thank God for the specialness of the time we had together.

We simply went outside. It was a still summer evening and we walked down to the church and sat outside in the stillness. I explained to the group that I wanted us to take the opportunity of being alone with God. I went on to say that whenever I was finding things were difficult, or I felt far away from God, or sad or very happy, then I would find a special place to be alone with God. I think they valued the private nature of what I was sharing with them—young people value honesty and self-disclosure from an adult very highly. Perhaps you might be able to share similar experiences of your time with God.

We took a Bible with us and looked up the passage from Luke that we were using earlier. I explained that I would pray each line and then leave a gap for them to put in any prayers they wanted to. I told them they could pray out loud or in their heads—whichever they felt most comfortable with. We began with, 'Father: May your holy name be honoured...' and then they added prayers asking God to help us honour him, in what we said and how we acted. They asked for help not to swear (although I hadn't mentioned that in the session). They thanked God for being so mighty and yet so humble. And so we went on, through each line pausing for prayers to be inserted at each point.

I had thought they probably wouldn't say much, if anything, but they all prayed out loud—something I counted as a small miracle! A time of prayer such as this does not need to be very long, but it can be very important to your group as they begin to learn about praying, both together and on their own. This is an important part in their Christian journey, developing life-long spiritual skills that they will need every day. Perhaps one day it will be part of the skill they teach their own children. At the end of the session give your group a feather each to take home. Explain that in the Personal Connections Sheet for this session there are some thoughts about prayer being like a feather and that they'll need their feathers to help them to fill it out. Give them the envelopes to keep their feathers in. These can be stuck into their folders so they don't get lost.

You need to end this session positively, either with refreshments or with a cheery farewell and reminder that the next session will be looking at the Church. Sometimes ending with quiet prayer can leave a group with a downbeat feeling, so try to make sure you always end on a positive note.

Seven

PERSONAL CONNECTIONS SHEET

Luke 11:1-4

One day Jesus was praying in a certain place. When he had finished, one of his disciples said to him, 'Lord, teach us to pray, just as John taught his disciples.' Jesus said to them, 'When you pray, say this: "Father: May your holy name be honoured; may your Kingdom come. Give us day by day the food we need. Forgive us our sins, for we forgive everyone who does us wrong. And do not bring us to hard testing."'

fold me now · · · · · · · · · · *fold me*

PERSONAL REFLECTIONS

CONNECTING VERSE

Be joyful always, pray at all times, be thankful in all circumstances. This is what God wants from you in your life in union with Christ Jesus.

1 Thessalonians 5:16-18

Prayer feathers

Prayer is a delicate thing. Sometimes like a feather it seems so fleeting and fragile. Yet a bird's wing is made of many feathers which enable the bird to fly. A prayer on its own might seem light and frail, but many prayers, like many feathers, are wings of communication with God. This week you were given a feather to help you think about the nature of prayer. When you pray you might like to hold your feather in your hand, remembering that, just as the feather would flutter if you let it go in the wind, so your prayers fly to God. Imagine your prayers joining other prayers: prayers you have said or thought, the prayers of others, prayers of the Holy Spirit on our behalf. Each one part of the wing of prayer to God.

Record your thoughts about your prayer time in the space.

Was it helpful to use the steps to prayer?

Six steps to prayer

Step 1 …

Step 2 …

Step 3 …

Step 4 …

Step 5 …

Step 6 …

Connecting with the Church

This session aims... to explore the earliest example of the Church mentioned in the Bible and to draw some lessons for ourselves as members of the Church today.

Before the session starts... prepare yourself by reading the material you will be using in the session. Prayerfully read through the Bible passage.

Prepare the room you will be using for the session. Have ready pencils and the session's Personal Connections Sheets for each member of the group, plain A4 sheets of paper and spare Bibles. You'll also need to copy the diagram on the Personal Connections Sheet onto a flip chart, or similar sized sheet of paper. Provide chunky coloured felt-tipped pens to write with and finally collect together some nice big pebbles, one for each of the group members, about the size of a ping pong ball or slightly larger.

First Connections

Welcome the group to the session. Answer any questions that may have arisen from the last session and briefly outline what you are going to be looking at this time.

Kick off the session by brainstorming types of groups that are 'close-knit' and exhibit a sense of community, for example, the local village football team, members of a band, an amateur dramatic group, a class at school, a tutor group, or a Christian Union. When you've thought of a good selection, choose one that the majority of your group knows well. Then, in small cells of two or three, make a list of the characteristics of that group. For example: friendly, caring, loyal. Are there any negative things about them? Are they a clique and unwelcoming to new people, for example?

Write the list of characteristics up on the flip chart or large sheet of paper in the appropriate box, allocating someone from each small cell to be the scribe and allowing plenty of discussion about the positive and negative aspects of the chosen group. Ensure that everyone has a chance to contribute, and that all the ideas get written down. They can then copy them onto their own diagram in their Personal Connections Sheets.

Bible Connections

Acts 2:42–47

Put the passage in its context by explaining that the events took place just after Pentecost. Pentecost is the Jewish festival of harvest and there would have been many visitors in Jerusalem at the time. Acts 2:1 shows us that the disciples were meeting together to celebrate this festival—remember that they were Jewish and therefore would have followed the Jewish calendar at this point in time. This particular festival of Pentecost would have fallen some time after Jesus had ascended into heaven. The Bible records that whilst they were gathered together they experienced a noise like wind filling the room and tongues of flame appeared to rest on each of their heads. The Bible explains how they were 'filled with the Holy Spirit and began to talk in other languages, as the Spirit enabled them to speak'. They had received the 'helper' promised to them by Jesus before his death and resurrection. The crowds, who had come to Jerusalem, from many different countries, were amazed to hear the disciples speaking in their own language. This event was the turning point for the disciples and sets the scene for the passage we are looking at in this session.

There is a great emphasis on the importance of community in Acts 2:44–45 and the disciples are portrayed as willingly putting their personal possessions at the disposal of their fellow Christians.

Read the passage together, or choose someone to read it (or use the cassette tape if you have made one).

Invite the group to select the four words that they feel best describe the way the disciples lived. For example: sharing... friendship... prayerfully... joyfully.

Bible Connections

Further Connections

Now turn back to the list of characteristics of a group which you did at the beginning of the session. Read through the passage again, this time pausing every time an example of community or fellowship is mentioned. Allocate another scribe for each small cell to write down the examples you identify, using a different colour felt-tipped pen, in the place indicated. How do they compare with the characteristics you identified with the first group? If they are similar, what does this say about the group you first thought about? If they are different, what conclusions would you draw? They can then copy these into their Personal Connections Sheets.

Go on to think about your own church situation. How does your own church community compare with the two diagrams you have created? Spend a few minutes sharing together what it is you most value about your church or fellowship group. What are the factors that make up a fellowship or community? Use your two lists to help you think about this. How does your own church measure up? What could you do about any areas which you feel are unsatisfactory? Most churches are far from perfect and young people are good at spotting the ways in which their own church falls short of the ideal, but encourage them also to think about where they fit into the picture. Do *they* measure up to the picture of the church community painted in this passage? They need to answer that question both in terms of the local church which they attend and also in terms of their own small group, meeting together as part of the church. Do they enjoy a sense of fellowship within the group? What do they as individuals perceive as their own role within the group? They can then fill in the final section on their Personal Connections Sheets.

At this point it would be good to take time to define what is meant by 'fellowship'. You might find it helpful to use a cross-shaped diagram to explain how Christians see fellowship in terms of a vertical sharing—a sharing with God, in that we have fellowship with Jesus and so a relationship with God himself; and also a horizontal sharing—a sharing across, a relationship with one another which is enhanced by our relationship with Jesus. To take the picture one step further, having drawn the horizontal and added the vertical, go on to explain that it is because of the cross that we can enjoy the fellowship of God and his Church. Point out that friendship in secular groups is not fellowship in this sense, because it does not have the cross at its heart.

Connecting With God

Hand out the pebbles, one for each member of the group. Use them to explain that each one of us is like a pebble in the building of God's Church—the individual stones that, when built together, make up the whole. Explain that God's Church is not made up of bricks and mortar, but people—the people of God. Each one of us is an important part of God's plan for his Church. Spend a few minutes studying the pebbles very carefully—encourage them to get to know their individual pebbles, looking for any peculiarities in it which might help them to identify it. Go round the group inviting them to say what they have noticed about their own pebble. Are any two the same? After a while put the pebbles together in a pile in the middle of the group. Can they find their own pebble in the pile? Give them a few minutes to do this. When everyone has found their own pebble, explain that, like the pebbles, each one of us is unique. Now invite them to build their pebbles into a simple wall. Work on the wall until each pebble seems to have its own place in the design. Go on to point out that, just as each individual stone in a building fits into the whole, so

God has a special place for each one of us in his Church where, together with others, we are made into a strong and visible building—the Church of God. Each individual stone in a building is nothing without its fellow stones—it would hardly be noticed, but together the stones make a powerful impact. This is God's purpose for us as his people—the stones of his building, making an impact in his world. In those early days in Jerusalem the people of God used the outward expressions of taking part in fellowship, of sharing in the fellowship meals and prayers and of sharing their belongings with one another to build up God's Church. How does the group think this relates to what they see in our churches today? Where might things be improved? If God calls us to share with each other for the common good, how might we do this? The groups I have worked with have come up with things like sharing our time, sharing our interests in the local community, caring for people in the church who are in need, cleaning the church, raising money for the church and so on. You might find your group thinks of things like sharing with the teaching in Sunday school, sharing responsibility for the lonely in the community or sharing in worship. The list is endless!

The Big Question

Here is the crucial question for this session:

What makes a group of people into a church?

As we have seen, the Church of God is not made of bricks and mortar, but of people. Each of us is the Church, not the Church of tomorrow as young people are often told, but of today. Young people are responsible for renewing the Church, for keeping it focused. If you want to strengthen your own understanding of this I recommend you purchase a copy of the Church of England report, *Youth A Part*. The theology section is particularly significant. The report recommends that young people be involved in the decision-making processes in their local church, through representation on its PCC or Council, and also in

more informal ways, and that young people be fully represented in the life of the church, in its public worship, in its secular identity and in its private life of housegroups and prayer. Ask your group what they think about this. Do they identify with the church in the way we have been describing, or do they identify only with the church as a building, or as represented by the minister or the older members of the congregation? If they could do something to change their own perception or the perception of others what would that 'something' be?

Concluding Connections

The aim of this section is to focus on our own role in the church to which we belong and to praise God for his provision for us as his people. There will also be the opportunity to ask for his help as we struggle to become more fully part of his 'building' in the world. Explain to the group that you are going to spend a few minutes in prayer, so they need to make sure that they are comfortable. Invite them to pick up their pebbles out of the wall you built earlier if they haven't already done so, and then give them a few minutes to write their name on their pebble. When they have done this invite them to hold their pebbles quietly in their hands. You might like to play some reflective music as you settle into this time of prayer together.

Begin by reminding the group how important they are as the individual stones in the 'building' of God's Church. After a pause go on to remind them how much it is part of God's unique plan for each of us to be a part of his building.

Pause again before reading the poem below. (The poem was written by a young person from Ducklington.)

Our New Church

We built a bonfire the other day
and crowded round to watch the blaze.
We read the Bible and discussed what
we had read.
That night we were the Church.
Not the building,
not the bricks and mortar,
but us.
The flesh and blood,
the Spirit within.
It was great!

Oli

Read the poem quietly, repeating it if you feel it is right to do so, and invite the group to pray silently. Then, creating pauses where you feel it appropriate, encourage them to ask God to reveal how he wants to work within their church fellowship, within his people who are his Church, and within their own lives. Finally, invite the group to ask God how he wants them to become more a part of the Church he is building. Remind the group of the pebbles they are holding, and how each individual is a stone in the building of God's Church.

At the end of the session invite your group to take the pebbles home with them as a reminder of how important they are to God's plan: they are the building blocks in God's kingdom.

Eight

Personal Connection Sheet

Acts 2:42-47

They spent their time in learning from the apostles, taking part in the fellowship, and sharing in the fellowship meals and the prayers. Many miracles and wonders were being done through the apostles, and everyone was filled with awe. All the believers continued together in close fellowship and shared their belongings with one another. They would sell their property and possessions, and distribute the money among all, according to what each one needed. Day after day they met as a group in the Temple, and they had their meals together in their homes, eating with glad and humble hearts, praising God, and enjoying the good will of all the people. And every day the Lord added to their group those who were being saved.

Personal Reflection

Think about your pebble, and think about how you are part of God's Church. Does that make you feel big and important or small and insignificant?

The crucial question this week was: What makes a group of people into a church?

What do you think makes people into a church, and how does your church measure up?

Connecting Verse

One by one, people will say, 'I am the Lord's.' They will come to join the people of Israel. They will each mark the name of the Lord on their arms and call themselves members of God's people.

Isaiah 44:5

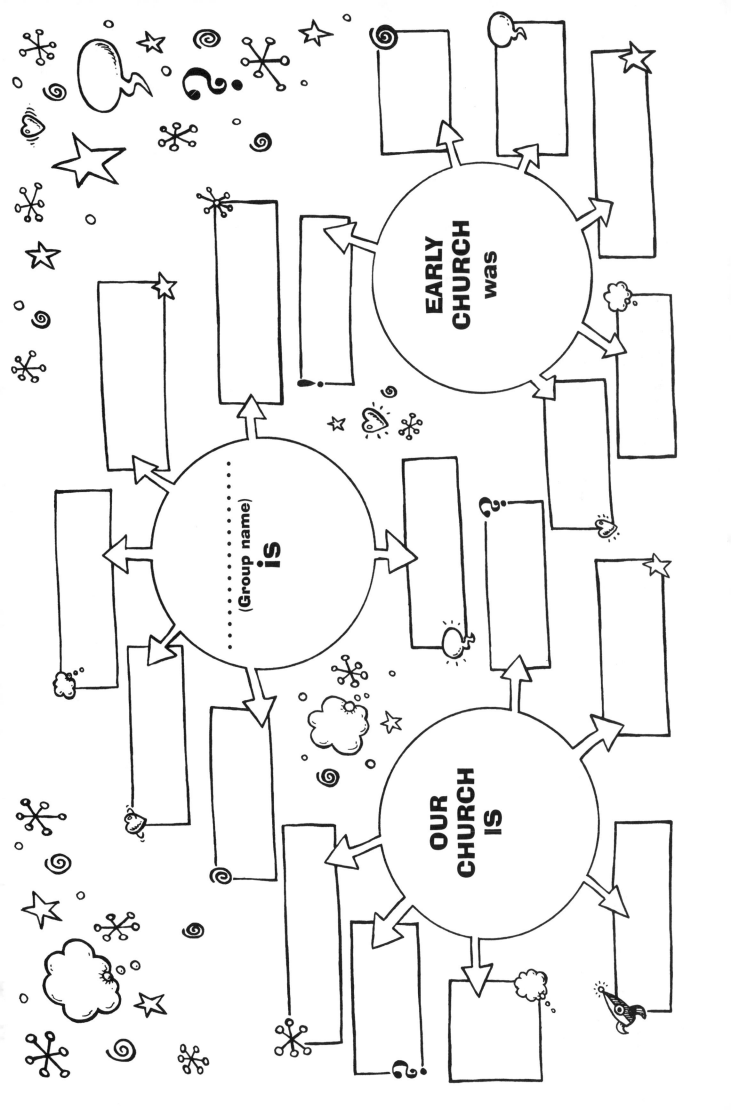

Confirming the Connection

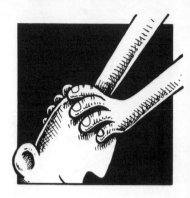

This session aims... to set out what is required of those preparing for confirmation in the Anglican Church. It is designed to give the candidate a fuller understanding of the vows they will make and provide the opportunity to reflect on their readiness to make this step of commitment.

The session is therefore optional if you are running this course for a group who are not preparing for confirmation. You might, however, still find the material of use as it sets out the fundamentals of Christian belief.

Before the session starts... prepare yourself by reading the material you will be using in the session. Prayerfully read the Bible passage.

Prepare the room you will be using for the session. Have ready pencils and the Personal Connections Sheets for each member of the group, plain A4 sheets of paper and spare Bibles. You'll also need three large sheets of plain paper, several hard-backed books and a small toy figure.

First Connections

Welcome the group to the session. Answer any questions that may have arisen from the last session and briefly outline what you are going to be looking at this time.

Start the session by asking the group to think about the things you might have to do or say to show your commitment to a particular group. Scouts or Guides would be a good example. The military services, the police force, or the medical professions would also be good examples of organizations where you would need to make promises of commitment before belonging. I'm sure your group will be able to think of more examples. Brainstorm the sort of promises you would need to make. It would be good to have personal examples you could give. The aim is to show that for certain things in life we need to think carefully about why we want to be identified with a particular group.

All Christians belong to God's Church, but within that Church people tend to feel comfortable worshipping God in a particular way, either because they grew up in a family that worshipped in that way, or because they became a Christian through a friend who did, or they discovered that that was the way they found most helpful when they became a Christian. Explain that the Church of England is part of the family of God, worshipping God in a particular way that has developed through the history of the Church in this country. Confirmation is a way of saying that you want to be a full member of the Church of England, but, of course, it is also much more than just saying you want to belong to a particular denomination.

Bible Connections
Ezekiel 36:25a, 26–28

The passage we are going to study to help us explore the heart of what confirmation means is one of the suggested readings for the Service of Confirmation.

Read out the passage. It's quite short so it could easily be read by a member of your group. Then go on to explain that this is a promise made by God to the people of Israel, but that it is also a promise which holds true for us today.

It is worth taking a few minutes to set Ezekiel in context. He is a fascinating prophet. He lived at the same time as Jeremiah and was one of those taken captive by the Babylonians in the first deportation in 597BC. Five years later, still in exile from the land he loved, he was called by God to be a prophet. He had a vision of a fiery cloud from the north containing a chariot drawn by four winged creatures. In the chariot was a throne and on the throne was a shining figure which flashed with a bright light, the dazzling light that showed the presence of God himself. In his vision Ezekiel was given a scroll containing messages for both the people in exile in Babylon and for the people of Jerusalem. The messages were a warning of God's judgment on the nation of Israel because the people had turned their backs on God and gone their own way. But, as well as a message of punishment, the message was also one of restoration, bringing the people back to God and giving them a new heart and a new way to worship through his Holy Spirit. This was a revolutionary message to a people who were used to worshipping God from afar, rather than experiencing him in a personal relationship.

It is easy to think of confirmation as something that we do, or even something that the Bishop does to us, and in some ways this is true—but, more than that, it is something that God does. Confirmation is a sacrament. One definition of a sacrament is that it is the outward and visible sign of an inward and spiritual grace—it is something that God does and we make a ceremony out of! This is the heart of what confirmation really is. It is the outward sign of what God is doing in our hearts. The Personal Connections Sheets for this session have a diagram of a heart for personal reflection. Invite the group to read the passage through again, quietly on their own, and then to fill in the heart diagram. They need to fill in the boxes, indicating what 'stone' things need to go out and what 'flesh' things need to move in. Explain that they can put one or more things in each space of the sheet. Give time for them to do this and then ask them to think about what difference it makes to our lives when God puts his Spirit into our hearts.

Further Connections

The first part of the Service of Confirmation requires the candidate to answer two sets of three questions, which are the renewal of their baptismal vows. As you go through the questions together it is important to point out that, when the candidate answers the questions, he or she is making a public promise; a promise which, if they were baptized as infants, was made for them on their behalf and now they are to make for themselves. It is a promise to God, a promise to the people of God (his Church), and a promise to themselves.

The first question is:

Do you turn to Christ?

Ezekiel knew that the only way for Israel to be restored was for the people to turn back to God. The same is true for us today. Invite the group to look at the things they put in the 'flesh' side of their heart diagram. Write their suggestions on a large sheet of paper. Your list will probably include love, peace, faith, joy and so on. Point out that these are all things that grow in us when God gives us the gift

of his Spirit. (Refer again to Galatians 5:22–23, the fruit of the Spirit.) When we promise to turn to Christ, God fulfils his promise to give us a new heart and a new mind. He takes away our heart of stone and puts his Spirit in us.

This is what we are asking for when we make the promise, 'I turn to Christ.'

The second question is:

Do you repent of your sins?

Turning towards God is not enough—we can know about Jesus, but still not be a Christian. A Christian is someone who has turned towards God and willingly asked him to forgive and accept them into his family. When we repent of our sins, we do an about-turn—we turn away from the wrong things in our lives and turn towards God. Invite the group to look at the things they put in the 'stone' side of their heart diagram. Write their suggestions on a large sheet of paper. Explain that these are the things they need to be sorry about. When we confess these things to God he wipes the slate clean so that we can forget all about them. Spend a few minutes in silence thinking about the things on the sheet. Perhaps there are other things that the individual members of the group might want to bring before God in the silence of their hearts. Aim to instil a sense of God's forgiveness rather than the heaviness of guilt.

When we promise to repent of our sins, God fulfils his promise continually to clean away the bad things in our lives. He gives us a new heart and a new mind. He takes away our disobedient heart of stone and puts his Spirit in us.

This is what we are asking for when we make the promise, 'I repent of my sins.'

The third question is:

Do you renounce evil?

Renouncing evil is part of the process of turning away from the wrong things in our lives and turning towards Christ. We cannot turn to face Christ and at the same time be facing towards evil. To renounce something is to turn your back on it and this is what each of us is asked to do when we become Christians.

Sometimes it is not easy to turn our backs on patterns of a lifetime (even a short lifetime!). Explain to the group that God doesn't expect us to be able to do this on our own. He provides his Spirit to help us to follow his laws and to keep his commands. In the passage in Ezekiel, God promises to put his Spirit in his people in order to help them to repent and renounce evil. When we pray for God continually to put his Spirit in us we are given the best defence ever for renouncing evil. When we are full of God's Spirit we will not be able to tolerate evil, and will be given the strength to renounce it.

We all face everyday evils and need to know how to combat them. Split the group into pairs and invite them to share one of the things on the 'stone' side of their heart diagram that they would like to combat. This exercise is very valuable as it teaches that it is right to be accountable to other Christians for the things we do wrong. It will encourage your group to think spiritually about their lives and to explore ways in which they might best live in a way that pleases God. Exploring the 'stones' in our hearts with others often helps us to know how to avoid them—something very pleasing to God!

When we promise to renounce evil, God fulfils his promise to put his Spirit in us to help us to live our lives his way.

This is what we are asking for when we make the promise, 'I renounce evil.'

The Bishop will now ask the candidates to declare their faith before God, saying:

You must now declare before God and his Church that you accept the Christian faith into which you were baptized, and in which you will live and grow.

Note the 'live and grow'! Point out that the Christian faith is like a journey and that reaching the point where we are able to declare our faith is a step on the way. As we reach this point where we identify ourselves as Christians, before God and his Church, in heaven and on earth, again there are three questions:

Do you believe and trust in God the Father who made the world?

Do you believe and trust in his Son Jesus Christ, who redeemed mankind?

Do you believe and trust in his Holy Spirit, who gives life to the people of God?

These questions, which we have been exploring in this course, are the same promises made at baptism. The service of baptism uses water to symbolize our acceptance into the family of God. In the passage from Ezekiel, God promises to sprinkle the people with clean water and so to cleanse them. Water is a very powerful symbol in the Bible. In the days of Ezekiel, for a tribal people, now settled, but displaced by an aggressive power, water was a vital commodity. In a dry land often subject to drought, water was very precious. It made the difference between life and death. Being able to wash with clean water from a tap would have been an unimaginable luxury. So the symbol chosen by God to bring his people back to himself was very powerful indeed. When Jesus chose to be baptized by John the Baptist in the River Jordan he was demonstrating this wonderful truth of his Father, that the precious water of baptism is a symbol of the living, spiritual water of life that only Jesus can give, to clean us, to revive us, and to give us new life in his Spirit.

The Service of Confirmation is the confirmation of the promises made at baptism. The answer to each of the three questions is the same, 'I believe and trust in him.' It is saying 'yes' to God, publicly saying we want to belong to God and to receive what he has promised us.

Further Connections

The Big Question

On a breakfast TV programme there is a slot called 'The big decision' where someone with a difficult decision to make records a short video of the issues involved and sends it to the programme. A panel then votes on what the person should decide to do. This has always struck me as a convenient way to avoid responsibility. We should all be responsible for our own decisions and prepared to live with the consequences!

So the Big Question this week is:

Will you decide to say 'yes' to God, and what will the consequence be?

Sometimes it seems easier for us as youth leaders to skip over the second part of this question. We are eager to see our young people make a commitment to God, but we don't always think through our responsibility to them for the decision they have made. Perhaps we secretly hope that we won't have to deal with the consequences! But when young people make the decision to be Christians, they are making a life-changing decision which will affect the rest of their lives. So we need to ensure that we, and they, are aware of what the consequences of that important decision might be. Invite the group to spend just five minutes brainstorming what those consequences may be—don't forget some positive consequences as well as the harder, negative ones! Write the suggestions down on a third sheet of paper.

Concluding Connections

When you have made your list you might find that the consequences seem more daunting than exciting! However, we are not making the decision in our own strength, but in God's. I am grateful to a friend of mine, Debbie North, for the idea used to draw this section together before God. Stand several hard-backed books up in a line in the middle of the group. The books represent the barriers to our Christian faith which we all face in life. Place your finger, or a toy figure, in front of the first book and, referring to the list of consequences you have made together, explain that this is what life is like. We stand in front of each decision we make in life and cannot see clearly what the consequence of our decision will be—because we do not know the future. God, however, can see down the line. He can see all the books, all the different situations we will meet, all the decisions we will have to make and, if we are willing to accept his Lordship of our lives, he promises to be there with us. Give time for reflection on the list of consequences and move the reflection into a time of prayer. Prayer is like throwing a pebble over the walls of the decisions we have to make in life. When we pray about the decisions set before us, God will show us the way through, even though we don't know what the consequences will be.

Lay the sheets of paper down on the floor together with the wall of books and use them as a focus for this prayer, based on the ASB Service of Confirmation:

Almighty and everliving God,
you give me new birth
in baptism by water and the Spirit,
and forgive all my sins.
Let your Holy Spirit rest upon me:
the Spirit of wisdom and understanding;
the Spirit of counsel and inward strength;
the Spirit of knowledge and true godliness;
and let my delight be in the fear of the Lord.

Amen.

Nine

PERSONAL CONNECTIONS SHEET

Ezekiel 36:25a, 26–28

'I will sprinkle clean water on you and make you clean... I will give you a new heart and a new mind. I will take away your stubborn heart of stone and give you an obedient heart. I will put my spirit in you and I will see to it that you follow my laws and keep all the commands I have given you. Then you will live in the land I gave your ancestors. You will be my people, and I will be your God.'

---

folding folding folding

PERSONAL REFLECTIONS

The decision you are being asked to make is not whether or not you want to be confirmed, but whether or not you choose to follow Christ and be a Christian.

When we decide to follow Christ there are likely to be some changes in our lives. Write out what you think these might be for you at the present time, and for the future.

CONNECTING VERSE

'The right time has come,' Jesus said, 'and the Kingdom of God is near! Turn away from your sins and believe the Good News!

Mark 1:15

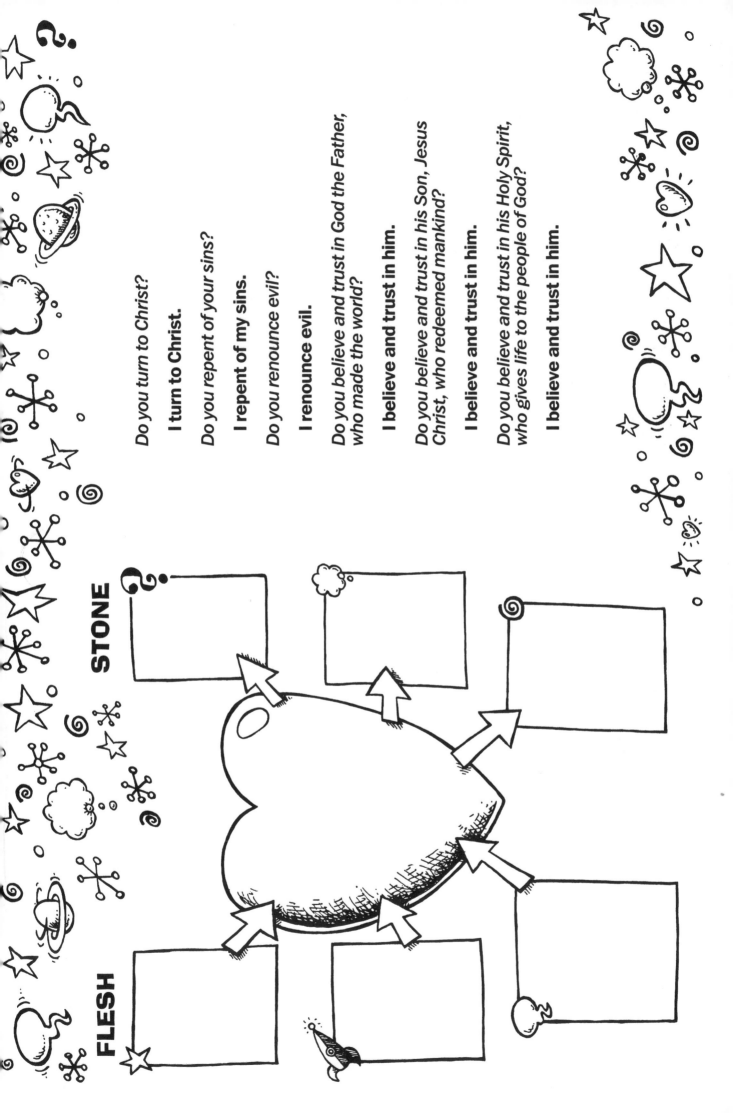

STONE

FLESH

Do you turn to Christ?

I turn to Christ.

Do you repent of your sins?

I repent of my sins.

Do you renounce evil?

I renounce evil.

Do you believe and trust in God the Father, who made the world?

I believe and trust in him.

Do you believe and trust in his Son, Jesus Christ, who redeemed mankind?

I believe and trust in him.

Do you believe and trust in his Holy Spirit, who gives life to the people of God?

I believe and trust in him.

Keeping up the Connection

This session aims... to look at how the sharing together in the sacrament of Holy Communion is an important way to keep up our connection with God.

Before the session starts... prepare yourself by reading the material you will be using in the session. Prayerfully read through the Bible passage.

Prepare the room you will be using for the session. Have ready pencils and the session's Personal Connections Sheets for each member of the group, plain A4 sheets of paper and spare Bibles. You'll also need some large sheets of plain paper, some bread and some wine or fruit juice, set out in an attractive way.

First Connections

Welcome the group to the session. Answer any questions that may have arisen from the last session/the Service of Confirmation and briefly outline what you are going to be looking at this time.

This session is intended to come after the Service of Confirmation if you are using the course for confirmation. I feel it is important to keep in touch with your group following a confirmation course and this session enables you to have an excuse to meet after the Confirmation has taken place. However, dealing as it does with the heart of our faith, it would be equally relevant before the Service of Confirmation or, indeed, for a group not preparing for confirmation.

Holy Communion. The Lord's Supper. Mass. Eucharist. Call it what you will. It's interesting to note how many words we use for this sacrament; it shows how important it is to our faith.

Start by explaining that this session is slightly special, in that it's going to be the last before the Service of Confirmation/the first after it—delete as appropriate! If you're not running this as a confirmation course make up some other reason why it's special! Go on to explain that this week we are going to explore how God invites us to keep up our connection with him by sharing a special meal with us.

First of all, brainstorm everything that a host or hostess would do to get ready for a special meal. For example, clean the house, choose the menu, buy the food, cook the food, choose drinks to go with the meal, lay the table, and so on. Write all the suggestions down on a large sheet of paper. Then on another sheet of paper do the same for the guests who have been invited to this special meal. For example, responding to the invitation, deciding what to wear, buying a bottle of wine or box of chocolates to take, having a bath, getting dressed, travelling to the venue and so on. You need to end up with two lists detailing what both a host and a guest have to do to get ready for a special meal. Set the lists on one side—you'll need them later.

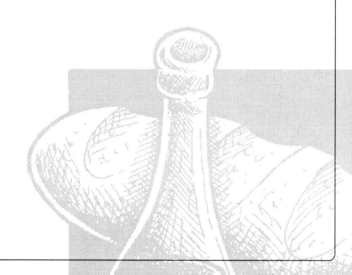

Bible Connections

Luke 22:7–20
or 1 Corinthians 11:23–26

The passage in Luke is an account of the Last Supper itself. However, you might prefer to use the teaching on the Lord's Supper from 1 Corinthians 11 which is more concise. This is the passage printed out in full on the Personal Connections Sheet. I have found the *Jesus of Nazareth* video quite powerful when teaching about this event, but you could just read the account from the Bible, or use your audio cassette if you made one. The *Dramatised Bible* can also be quite a good way to present the passage.

This passage has to be approached from its Jewish roots which are vibrant and alive and can add much to the understanding of our Christian faith.

The Jewish festival of Passover spans an eight-day period and is a time of celebration and remembrance for the time when God saved the Jewish people from captivity in Egypt. The festival itself may actually go back further, probably being in earliest times a merging of two spring festivals, the agricultural festival for the harvesting of crops and the nomadic festival of thanksgiving for the flock, where the firstborn of the flock was killed as a thank offering. After the exodus, Passover became the festival of redemption.

Remind the group of the slavery game you played in Session Three and how it illustrated the concept of redemption—a way of buying the freedom of a slave. The story of how God rescued his people from slavery forms the first twelve chapters of the book of Exodus and is well worth reading. You might like to précis the story for your group, ending with the story of the death of the firstborn before the escape from Egypt.

The feast of Passover gets its name from this story; it is a play on words as the angel of God 'passed over' the houses of the people of Israel, sparing their firstborn from death. The people were to sacrifice a lamb and put its blood on the doorposts of their houses as a secret sign so the angel of God would know to pass over the house. Then they were to cook and eat the lamb, together with bitter herbs, probably chicory and endive, as these are native to Egypt. These would remind them of the bitterness of their time in Egypt. They were to make bread without yeast (unleavened bread), which is quick to prepare. This was to remind them that they would have to leave Egypt quickly. God commanded them to celebrate the Passover every year as a way of remembering what God did for them that night. In this way the Jewish people keep up their connection with God.

So here in Luke we read of Jesus in Jerusalem, celebrating the festival of Passover with his disciples. The breaking of the bread and the sharing of the cup would have been familiar to the disciples—it was part of the Jewish ceremony. But Jesus turns it into something extraordinary. He makes a new ceremony out of it by explaining that this is a new Passover, a new redemption is coming, written in his blood. With his body he will pay the price to set everyone free from their slavery. With his words, in this symbolic way, Jesus predicts his death on the cross and his resurrection. He uses the wine as a symbol of the pouring out of his blood in order to seal God's covenant. A covenant is the promise of an agreement made between two people. When God rescued the people of Israel from Egypt he made a covenant with them: that he should be their God and they should be his people. Jesus makes a new covenant, a new promise, that each one of us can be rescued from spiritual death and find our way back to God through Jesus' death and resurrection. Our part of the agreement is that we are to believe what he has done for us.

Further Connections

The Jewish roots of Christianity are very hard for young people to understand and even harder for them to see what it's all got to do with them. To help them make the connection split the group into pairs and ask each pair to think of a question either about the Passover or about the Last Supper that they would like to put to the rest of the group. Use the Bible to explore the answers to the questions together. If you get stuck don't forget to take the question to someone who might be able to help you find the answer. Try to get all the group to work on these difficult issues. Remember that, although you may know more than they do, they will often have insights that you may not even have considered. As they explore the two celebrations, the celebration of Passover and the Lord's Supper, create two lists of their findings side by side on a large sheet of paper. Then compare the two lists

and see in what ways they connect together. The points you need to cover are:

• *The first covenant and the second covenant are linked. Jesus chose the Passover meal as the springboard for the new covenant—it wasn't a chance happening.*

• *The bitter herbs of pain are symbols of what Jesus had to suffer to pay the price to release us from our slavery.*

• *The new covenant is for everyone not just the Jewish people.*

• *The new covenant is based, not on man-made rules, but on the great rule of love. We claim the promises of Jesus when we believe and trust in him.*

Connecting With God

Go back to the lists for hosts and guests you made in the First Connections section. Explain that when a church holds a service of Holy Communion, it is not the church inviting you to attend but God. It was Jesus who said, 'Do this in memory of me.' God is the host of this special meal and we are the guests he invites. Now let's go back to the lists and look at the connections we can make. Split the group into small cells of two or three and invite them to use their Personal Connections Sheets to make some connections between God as host to this special meal and the list of things they decided a host does to get ready.

Ask them to relate each point they made about the host to God. For example, if they said the host would have to invite the guests, then the questions are: How does God invite us? Who does he invite? What preparations did the group say would have to be made? What preparations did God have to make? What preparations does he make today? And so on. I have found this to be a very enlightening exercise with the groups I have worked

with. One group came up with a brilliant connection, pointing out that the host has to make sure the glasses are clean before pouring wine into them, and Jesus refers to us as wine skins, needing to be made new. God as the host has to make us new in order for us to receive the new wine he wants to give us! Now that is deep theological thinking—it's so exciting to be part of a group like that! I hope you have fun!

When you have looked at the list for the host, do the same for the guests. If we are the guests, what do we need to do in order to come to this very special meal with God as the host?

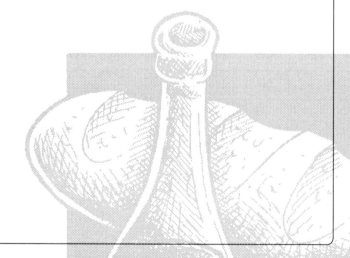

The Big Question

God invites us to his special meal because he wants us to remember all he has done for us, to confirm the connection he has made with us and the connection we have made with him.

The Big Question is:

Will we keep up the connection?

In the Church of England at the present time the invitation to receive the sacraments of bread and wine are available to all those confirmed into the Anglican Communion and usually extended to all those who love and serve the Lord in other denominations. You are probably aware that much debate is going on to try to make this as inclusive as possible, whilst at the same time maintaining the seriousness of the invitation. Celebrating Holy Communion is not an optional extra for a Christian. We cannot be Christians in isolation. We cannot celebrate this meal alone. Holy Communion is the symbolic heart of the Christian faith. It is an important way to keep up our connection with what God has done for us. So what does the church that your group is connected to feel about the importance of this special meal and how is it celebrated? Your group might have members who have backgrounds in differing traditions who will be able to contribute to a discussion on ways of celebrating Holy Communion. How often do the group feel we should come together to celebrate our faith in this way?

Concluding Connections

Set out some bread and wine, or red grape juice, on a table in the centre of the group as a focus for drawing this session together in a small act of devotion. You might prefer to use the elements symbolically, or to share them together as an *agape* meal. Alternatively, you could arrange to hold a very short Service of Holy Communion at this point. You need to talk to your minister about this if you are not ordained.

I have used some words from an order of service for Holy Communion written by William Barclay for this *agape* meal. They are printed on the Personal Connections Sheets so that each person has their own copy. They are the words of invitation to the Communion table.

Come, not because you are strong, but because you are weak.

Come, not because any goodness of your own gives you a right to come, but because you need mercy and help.

Come, because you love the Lord a little and would like to love him more.

Come, because he loved you and gave himself for you.

Lift up your hearts and minds above your cares and fears and let this bread and wine be to you the token and pledge of the grace of the Lord Jesus Christ, the love of God and the fellowship of the Spirit, all meant for you if you will receive them in humble faith.

William Barclay, The Lord's Supper, SCM Press, 1967

Read each line slowly, allowing the words to sink in. In what areas are we weak and need to be strong? In what ways do we need mercy and help? In what ways would we like to know God more?

If you are wanting to treat this act of devotion as an *agape* meal you can then go on to share the bread and wine with the group. If you are not ordained the elements will not be consecrated. It is nevertheless a very special way to finish your time together, using ordinary bread and red grape juice, or wine, as a way of showing the group how vital a part this is of keeping up their connection with God. An *agape* meal provides an ideal ending to the course, whether you were using it for confirmation preparation or not, and is also a wonderful way to start your life together as members of God's family after the Service of Confirmation.

Personal Connections Sheet

1 Corinthians 11:23–26

For I received from the Lord the teaching that I passed on to you: that the Lord Jesus, on the night he was betrayed, took a piece of bread, gave thanks to God, broke it, and said, 'This is my body, which is for you. Do this in memory of me.' In the same way, after the supper he took the cup and said, 'This cup is God's new covenant, sealed with my blood. Whenever you drink it, do so in memory of me.' This means that every time you eat this bread and drink from this cup you proclaim the Lord's death until he comes.

---

folding on up

Personal Reflections

Mark yourself on the line

No commitment to God — Total commitment to God

Connecting Verse

The Spirit and the Bride say, 'Come!' ... Come, whoever is thirsty; accept the water of life as a gift, whoever wants it.   **Revelation 22:17**

Come, not because you are strong, but because you are weak.

Come, not because any goodness of your own gives you a right to come, but because you need mercy and help.

Come, because you love the Lord a little and would like to love him more.

Come, because he loved you and gave himself for you.

Lift up your hearts and minds above your cares and fears and let this bread and wine be to you the token and pledge of the grace of the Lord Jesus Christ, the love of God and the fellowship of the Spirit, all meant for you if you will receive them in humble faith.

William Barclay

What God does

What the host does

What we do

What the guest does

Conclusion

If you are not planning to continue running the group meetings at the end of the course, then you need to think of a really good activity to finish. I would recommend some kind of social event, fairly low key; a meal perhaps, either at someone's house or better still at a restaurant. Most restaurants will do a fixed price meal, so all you need to do is write a letter to parents, setting out the arrangements and the cost, collect the money before you go and pay the bill at the end of the meal. A little gift for each member of the group and a short speech about how wonderful they are will ensure an ending that is memorable and positive.

If you are planning to continue meeting with the group there are three main recommendations which are worth thinking about in order to ensure your plans are successful.

First of all, it is important to focus your plans with some background reading. I highly recommend *Youth A Part*, the recent Church of England report on young people and the Church. The whole report proves fascinating reading, but the theology section is particularly good, helping you to think in theological terms about youth work. It really helps you to focus your mind on why you want to work with young people, what you are looking to achieve and what God's role is in what you are doing.

As you read think about the reasons why your group wants to continue meeting and what will draw the young people together. Answer these questions as honestly as you can. You see, unless you can see God's hand in your group, then your enthusiasm, however well intended, will wane very quickly. Nothing is worse than a group that just trundles on with no real aim and which no one really enjoys.

Secondly, try to organize a Personal Connections Partner for each member of your group. Ideally this should be an adult of the same sex as the young person with good listening skills and a rapport with young people. It doesn't necessarily need to be someone who is young and trendy, just someone to share in the ups and downs of a young Christian's life, both spiritually and in a wider social context. There will be some members of your group for whom a Personal Connections Partner is not workable, but there will be others for whom it works really well. It seems to work best when the adults are either those without children themselves, whether single or married, or those whose children have left home. Age doesn't seem to be particularly relevant. Match the young people on a one to one basis with each adult, and ensure that there is no pressure on the part of the young person to continue if they don't want to.

Keep in contact yourself with the supporting adults and encourage them to pray for the young people. It seems to work well if a casual social contact is formed, for instance occasionally meeting over coffee or lunch. The aim is to provide the young people with prayer support and, where appropriate, with practical help—even if that's no more than someone to sit next to in church.

Finally, plan a residential event every six months or so. This needs be no more than one night away, and it doesn't have to be far away from your home. The act of planning and going away together has an amazingly strengthening effect on the group which will prolong the life of the group and build up their support of one another. Make sure that you have planned some kind of activity when you arrive, even if it is just cooking a meal together, and have some kind of discussion and time with God planned for the evening. You could get some activity ideas from the many books available on the subject, but you can't beat planning your own programme. Try to include a biblical focus appropriate to the group and spend some time in quiet reflection, perhaps with a meditation, music or some art materials or pens and paper for creative writing. Encourage the group to use their artistic creations to worship God, whether through art and writing, music and movement or prayers and silence.

One final point: it is impossible to run a group on your own; it takes far too much energy and commitment. So work towards building a team of volunteers around you. Train them if necessary—look out for youth training days happening in your area. Allow them to come and be part of the group with no commitment until they feel able to contribute. Above all get the church praying for you and the group. Merely including the young people in the intercessions during the Sunday service is not enough, there should be a commitment to pray built into the prayer times of individuals within the church family. Remember not to neglect your own spiritual needs. Allow the Holy Spirit to build you up through Bible study, fellowship, Holy Communion and prayer.

Most of all have fun, I'm sure you will!

Resources

Malcolm Goldsmith, *Knowing Me Knowing God*, Triangle/SPCK, 1994

General Synod Working Party, *Youth A Part*, National Society/Church House Publishing, 1996

John Mallison, *Growing Christians in Small Groups*, Scripture Union, 1989